Lidingo

Memories of the small Swedish haven
which 200 girls called 'home'
after the Holocaust

by **Chana (Igell) Mantel**

translated by: **Edward Levine**
edited by: **Ruth Steinberg**

Machon Yachdav
Jerusalem
5758 (1998)

First Edition, 1998

Paperback Edition
ISBN 978-1-68025-452-5

Design and layout by Rivka Rotenberg

Distributed by:
FELDHEIM PUBLISHERS
POB 43163 / Jerusalem, Israel

208 Airport Executive Park
Nanuet, NY 10954
www.feldheim.com

Distributed in Europe by:
LEHMANNS
+44-0-191-430-0333
info@lehmanns.co.uk
www.lehmanns.co.uk

Distributed in Australia by:
GOLDS WORLD OF JUDAICA
+613 95278775
info@golds.com.au
www.golds.com.au

Printed in USA

Lidingo

Contents

Lidingo in Perspective

by **Rav Shlomo Wolbe** *Shlita*

This book takes us back to the period following the defeat of Nazi Germany in the Second World War, when the destruction of European Jewry was revealed in all its horror. The gates of the ghettos and the death camps swung open and the survivors emerged: slave laborers bereft of their families, sick, despairing people, men and women, young and old, broken in body and in spirit. It was the fulfillment of the verse "For your ruin is as vast as the sea, who can heal you?" (Lamentations 2:13) In a humanitarian gesture, the Swedish government opened its doors to twenty thousand refugees, mostly women. With G-d's help, a school for girls was opened in Lidingo, a suburb of Stockholm. Approximately one hundred girls had the privilege of being educated and rehabilitated in this oasis, in the midst of the terrible desolation faced by the survivors.

Lidingo was permeated with a wonderful atmosphere of love and faith, Torah knowledge and closeness [to G-d]. Divine providence sent faithful messengers to Lidingo: **Rav Binyamin Zeev Jacobson** and his wife, the **Rebbetzin**, of blessed, saintly memory. Rav Jacobson was a well-known personality in orthodox European Jewry. He was the rav of the Machzikei HaDas community in Copenhagen. He possessed boundless love for his fellow Jews, great wisdom, and was a superb speaker. The Rebbetzin had been a pupil in Berlin of the outstanding educator, Dr. Deutschlander. (Dr. Deutschlander went on to found the Bais Yaakov movement together with Sara Schenirer.) The Rebbetzin was a deep thinker and a magnificent teacher. Wherever she lived, she gained renown for her classes on Tanach: in Hamburg, Berlin, and Copenhagen. Rav Jacobson's family came to Stockholm when the majority of Danish Jewry succeeded in fleeing after the German occupation of their country. He then served as the director of the Stockholm branch of the Vaad

HaHatzalah of the American Agudath Harabbanim. Rebbetzin Jacobson assumed the post of director of the new school and moved to Lidingo, leaving her family in Stockholm. From time to time, the family would visit Lidingo, and the Rav's presence there was always an impressive event. The girls were devoted to the Rebbetzin. She consoled them for all they had suffered, and infused them with fine *middos*, faith and trust in G-d, dedication to Torah, knowledge, and self-confidence.

Also from Heaven was the presence of a young, Torah observant family in Stockholm, that of **Nissan Igell**, of blessed memory. Nissan was a high school teacher, with an academic degree. The Swedish authorities, who maintained the school during its first years, were happy to appoint him administrator of the school. **Mrs. Igell**, his wife, served as housemother and cared for all the girls' needs. There were other teachers in Lidingo as well, each of whom made an important contribution to the institution. Even someone who was close to the institution and taught there, such as myself, was always impressed by the serious, studious atmosphere and wonderful spirit that reigned in Lidingo. What we did not know about was the terrible burden of memories from the past and the profound sorrow over the loss of their families borne by the girls. Thus we were unaware of the extent of the self-sacrifice on the part of Rebbetzin Jacobson and Mrs. Igell, who helped each of these emotionally traumatized girls, comforting them and rehabilitating them. This intimate side of the "Lidingo girls" is presented in this book.

And wonder of wonders: today, the Lidingo girls are grandmothers, thank G-d, but they still are bound together like actual sisters. This fact alone attests like one hundred witnesses to the unique nature of the school in Lidingo. It therefore is appropriate for the story of Lidingo to be recorded in book form. We thank the author for the effort she expended in successfully producing a valuable documentary volume.

Introduction

It was only after I completed the writing of this book and reread the text that I discovered the true magnitude of the phenomenon known as Lidingo. I had heard a great deal from my parents, especially from my mother, Mrs. Nina Igell, about the wonders of Lidingo, but it did not have a profound effect upon me until I interviewed the alumni, the Lidingo girls, most of whom live in *Eretz Yisrael.* These women, who have established wonderful families and are respected members of society in their communities, are a living testimony to the extraordinary success of the Lidingo spirit on the one hand, and the strength of human will power on the other.

In order to understand the magnitude of this success, we must recall that these girls came to Lidingo after undergoing all the horrors of the Holocaust, but nevertheless managed to overcome the terrible effects of their wartime experiences. Due to their faith in the Almighty, and thanks to the education they received in Lidingo, they became happy women who radiate a belief and trust in G-d obvious to all who meet them. As I began to record this story, I felt very small in comparison with the spiritual and moral greatness of these women. Their stories were treated with the greatest respect. I sought to remain faithful to their words, in order to give as accurate a picture as possible. I was unable, however, to conceal my amazement at the dedication of the staff of this unique institution, and their ability to deal with the diverse range of problems facing their young charges.

I wish to thank all those who aided me in the preparation of this book: the "Lidingo girls", who willingly spent so many hours of their time talking, telling their stories, and offering valuable advice; my mother, Mrs. Nina Igell, who provided her unique perspective on this shining chapter of Jewish history; my brother-in-law, Rav Yehuda

Sheinberger, who gave much needed assistance and support; and my dear husband, Shlomo Yosef Mantel, without whose help, support, and encouragement this book could not have been written. Finally, I would like to offer my heartfelt thanks to a special individual, great in thought and faith, **Rav Shlomo Wolbe** *shlita*, who conceived the idea of an orthodox girls' home for refugees in Sweden and saw it to fruition, for his encouragement and support of the publication of this book.

Special thanks to the Yachdav Institute and its directors, Rav Moshe Fogel, who initiated the publication of the book, and Rav Yechezkel Fogel, for his thoughtful editing and technical expertise. No effort or expense was spared to produce a readable and aesthetically pleasing volume, and for this I am grateful.

This book is dedicated to the blessed memory of my saintly father, **Reb Nissan Yaakov Igell**, who administered the institution in Lidingo on behalf of the Swedish government with unlimited faithfulness and dedication. His refinement and commitment to Torah were a unique phenomenon in Sweden. After settling in *Eretz Yisrael*, he devoted his time to the study and support of Torah. May his memory be a blessing.

Kislev 5756 (1996)
Chana Mantel

Rav Shlomo Wolbe Shlita and the Lidingo girls.
In the center: Rebbetzin Jacobson, *Morah* Chaya and Mrs. Nina Igel

Prologue

The ringing of the telephone shattered the silence in Mrs. Igell's study.

"Hello? I have a telegram here from Brooklyn, New York, for a Miss Pashat, Lidingo - is that you?"

As it later turned out, the telegram was actually addressed to "*Mishpachat* Lidingo," Hebrew for "the Lidingo family." But the phone connection was terrible, and the best the poor operator could do with the unfamiliar syllables was "Miss Pashat".

"Yes," said Mrs. Igell quickly, "This is *mishpachat* Lidingo. Can you read me the telegram, please?"

"Certainly. It says, `I'm engaged. Raizy.'"

"Oh, thank you! Thank you so much!"

As she hung up the phone, Mrs. Igell was overcome with excitement.

Despite her Swedish-bred restraint, she could not check the tears which suddenly filled her eyes. Through G-d's infinite kindness, another of her girls, their girls, was engaged.

"I must write to Raizy right away, G-d willing, to wish her *mazal tov* and ask her about her fiance," she thought happily. She headed straight for the dining room where dozens of girls where eating lunch, eager to share the good news with them.

"Girls!" she called, hardly able to make herself heard over the clamor of cutlery, plates, and non-stop conversation that arose from all sides.

"Girls, I have some wonderful news for you!" she announced.

It worked like a charm. Curious, they all turned towards her in delicious anticipation.

"Mazal tov, everybody! Raizy is engaged!"

Mrs. Igell was instantly surrounded by a buzzing circle of excited girls and bombarded with questions.

"Who's her fiance?"

"When did it happen?"

"How did it happen?"

"When did you find out?"

All around there were kisses, hugs, and tears. Raizy, their sister, was engaged. When would it be their turn?

The front of the "Lidingo House"

Lidingo

Who was the "Lidingo family" with its dozens of daughters? Where did they live, and why had Raizy cabled them from overseas to inform them of her engagement?

Lidingo is an island west of Stockholm, off the coast of the Baltic Sea. Visible from the top of the Kaknastornet tower in Stockholm and connected to the city by a bridge, it is easily accessible by train or car. In the years following the Second World War, this picturesque resort town was home to an amazing chapter in Jewish history, one which left its mark on the participants for years to come.

During the war, an unassuming house called Fiskarudden in Lidingo's Elfvik neighborhood had served as a dormitory for young Norwegian freedom fighters, undergoing combat training in neutral Sweden under orders from the Norwegian government-in-exile in London. From there, they would go on to join their country's fighting forces in England.

Despite its unlikely history, after the war Fiskarudden became home to a group of Jewish girls who had survived the Holocaust and found shelter in Sweden.

The house itself was not especially attractive, but the surroundings were breathtaking. After the girls moved in in the fall of 1945, they enjoyed their own private beach in the summer, and an enormous ice skating rink when the nearby bay froze over in the winter. On moonlit winter nights, the snow covered grounds were a scene of almost fairy tale beauty. Yet, beautiful and conveniently situated as it was, this was not what made Lidingo special; it was the the warmth of authentic Judaism which, thanks to a team of dedicated educators, pervaded the "Lidingo family" in Elfvik in the postwar years, providing new life and new hope for dozens of Jewish girls who had survived the inferno of the Holocaust.

Beginnings

Summer, 1945.

Rav Shlomo Wolbe, representative of the Vaad HaHatzalah in Sweden, had spent a bone racking day traveling to the refugee camp in Doversdorp, where, he had been told, he would find survivors of the concentration camps. When he arrived in the heat of midday, he was readily granted permission to visit the camp and its inmates. As he approached the dining room, he touched his hand to the doorpost, searching for something which would tell him a great deal about the nature of the camp. When he did not find it, he stepped into the room.

He wore a dark suit and hat, and had not only a beard, but *peyos* as well; typical rabbinic garb, but an unusual sight in a room whose doorpost lacked so basic a religious article as a *mezuza*.

The girls were busily engaged in eating - and hiding - food, when one of them noticed the newcomer. "Look!" she cried, "A *Yid!* A Jew! *Tatte!*" Heads shot up and eyes opened wide. It really *was* a Jew, a real Jew, just like before the war.

Rochke, one of the older girls, was the first to burst into tears.

Within minutes, the others followed. The soup was abandoned, the petty quarrels forgotten. How on earth had a bearded Jew wandered into their dining room? Where could he have come from? Hadn't the Germans killed them all?

The rav was speechless, and his eyes glistened with tears. What terrible sufferings these Jewish daughters must have endured!

Moments later, the camp director arrived. Yes, he told Rav Wolbe, the girls were from the concentration camps and yes, they were all Jewish.

Were they religious? He honestly did not know; no one had thought to ask. Jewish traditions were not observed in the camp, and everyone was free to behave as she pleased. When Rav Wolbe commented on their emotional reaction to the sight of a Jew with beard and *peyos*, the director told him, "It must remind them of home."

Rav Wolbe had brought along some kosher sandwiches for his lunch.

When he asked the girls where he could wash his hands for bread, they brought him water, and stood clustered around him as as he washed and recited the appropriate blessings. When he finished, he looked up and, to his surprise, saw that they were in tears once again. How long had it been since any of them had washed *netilas yadayim* and made the blessings, or seen another Jew do so?

These too were the ravages of war, no less than the physical illnesses being treated in compassionate Swedish hospitals.

"Enjoy your meal," he said softly, trying to hide the moisture in his eyes. He knew that he could not possibly leave these girls behind in Doversdorp, where they would be taken in by well-meaning but non-Jewish Swedish families, and thereby lost to the Jewish people forever. He waited out in the corridor until they had finished eating.

When they were done, he asked to speak to the girls who had come from the concentration camps in Poland. Twelve girls gathered around the rav, eager to speak with the man who reminded them of their lost homes, and happy to answer his questions about their lives and backgrounds.

"Dear girls," the rav began. He paused, searching for the right words. The girls listened expectantly. "I thank G-d for the privilege of seeing so many Jewish daughters who were saved from the inferno." Their tears, so close to the surface now, began to flow.

"Dear girls, with G-d's help, you will soon be able to attend a new school with dormitory facilities, run in accordance with Jewish law and tradition. Those who are interested can register right now."

A short line formed: Shoshana, Chana, Sorke, and a few others. They were terribly excited. Could it really be true? They had had their fill of promises...

When Rav Wolbe met these girls in Doversdorp, there was not, as yet, a religious girls' school in Sweden. But he fully intended to see to it that there would be one, and as soon as possible.

* * *

When Rav Wolbe called Rav Binyamin Zeev Jacobson, as soon as he stepped off the train in Stockholm, he already had the kernel of a plan. He asked that an urgent meeting of the Vaad HaHatzalah be convened, so that he could relate what he had seen in Doversdorp. That same evening, he addressed the Vaad in a voice charged with emotion.

"We cannot abandon those girls in Doversdorp! They need a school and a home. It's up to us to see to it that they receive a Torah-true education!" he insisted.

The Vaad members were quick to point out the unfortunate realities of life in Sweden. "R. Shlomo, what are you saying?" they protested, "We can't fight Dr. Ehrenpreis. As soon as he gets wind of the idea he'll do everything in his power to stop you. What's more, the

Swedish government will never allow it. It's a beautiful idea, but it's just a dream."

What they said was true. Dr. Marcus Ehrenpreis was the rabbi of the influential Reform Jewish congregation in Stockholm, and he would never agree to such a scheme, and nothing could be done without government approval in any case.

But Rav Wolbe would not be deterred. "We will because we must! It's unthinkable to leave those girls in Doversdorp on their own!"

"R. Shlomo, what you're asking is impossible."

"These girls are going to have a religious school! With G-d's help, we will succeed!" As far as Rav Wolbe was concerned, the discussion was over.

The *Vaad's* concern for the future of the girls in Doversdorp won them over to Rav Wolbe's position. Imbued with his determination and fired by his enthusiasm, they decided to submit a memorandum to the Swedish government. Composed by Rav Wolbe, it requested permission to establish a school for concentration camp survivors in Sweden. Together with Rav Eliezer Berlinger of Malmo, Rav Wolbe presented it in person, and explained how very urgent the projected school was for the girls in question.

A few days later, the Ministry of Foreign Affairs called the *Vaad* to arrange a meeting with Rav Wolbe and Rav Jacobson. When they arrived, the Ministry official's first question proved to be a pleasant surprise.

"Exactly how many schools do you want to open?" he asked.

The question was hardly what they had expected. "For the time being, one," was their immediate reply.

"Fine," said the Ministry official, "We'll keep our eyes open for a suitable location. As soon as we have something, we'll let you know." True to their word, the Ministry contacted the *Vaad* just a few days later. A promising site for the new school had been found in a town called Lidingo. A representative of the *Vaad HaHatzalah* was asked to come and approve the building.

In the meantime, the largely Reform official Swedish Jewish community learned of the *Vaad's* plans to open a strictly orthodox school for girls near Stockholm. Dr. Ehrenpreis, Stockholm's Reform rabbi, did everything in his power to sabotage the project, calling on all of his own and his congregation's long-standing government connections.

Reinforcing the refugees' Jewish identity through institutions like the proposed school could lead to a new wave of anti-Semitism, they argued; instead, the government should encourage the girls' speedy assimilation into the local non-Jewish community.

But it seemed that Divine providence was on the side of the new school. The activities of Dr. Ehrenpreis and his followers were carried out clandestinely, to prevent the *Vaad* from interfering. However, Mr. Bernstein, assistant cantor of the Reform temple in Stockholm, saw what was happening, and quietly arranged to meet with Rav Wolbe and Rav Jacobson at a local train station. When he told them of Dr. Ehrenpreis' doings, immediate steps were taken to counteract the damage. Rav Pinchas Wohlgelernter, emissary of the American *Agudath Harabbanim* to the Stockholm *Vaad*, stepped into the fray. He made the rounds of the government officials, persuading them to keep their promises to the *Vaad*. Despite the vicious slanders heaped upon him by Dr. Ehrenpreis and his congregation, he persisted in his efforts until the new school in Lidingo, with the full sanction of the Swedish government, was an accomplished fact.

Lidingo opened its doors on the first day of *Selichos*, 1945. The twelve Polish girls Rav Wolbe had met in

Doversdorp were its first students. Within a short time, Lidingo, both school and home to many homeless girls, would become one of Sweden's model educational institutions.

Rav Wohlgelernter remained a close friend of Lidingo, ever ready to extend vital financial and spiritual support to the administration, staff, and students. There were others as well who spared no effort to help Lidingo. Among them were R. Goodman from England, and Rav Boruch Kaplan, founder of New York's Bais Yaakov Seminary, who later helped a number of girls settle in the United States.

R. Yisrael Chasdan and his wife, Leah, also played a special role in Lidingo. They had lived in Sweden before the outbreak of the war, and were instrumental in helping the Jacobson family adjust to their new surroundings when they arrived from Denmark. The

The girls after their arrival at Lidingo.
In the center: Reb Nisan Igel, his wife Nina, and *Mora* Ahuva

Lidingo girls remember R. Chasdan for his warmth and utter devotion to his fellow man; nothing gave him greater plesasure than helping others. His home was always open to Holocaust survivors, some of whom lived with the family for periods upwards of a year. His Yiddish was flawless, and his Hebrew excellent. A collection of humorous essays by R. Chasdan entitled "*Lachen fun Tzorres*" (Laughing at Troubles) expressed his attitude towards his own problems; the problems of others, however, were afforded meticulous care. The Lidingo girls were frequent visitors at the Chasdan home, and the Chasdans often spent *Shabbos* in the school, where R. Chasdan's magnificent rendition of traditional Jewish songs added meaning and beauty to the day.

But the bulk of the burden of caring for the girls and bringing them back to Judaism fell to Rav Binyomin Zeev Jacobson who, together with Rabbetzin Jacobson, took on the management of the school and dormitory.

Alone and friendless, traumatized by the events of the war, the girls found themselves in a foreign country, forced to contend with a hopelessly foreign language. It was Rav Jacobson who was able to make them feel that finally, there were people who truly cared about them and loved them.

Years later, many still remembered their first meeting with the Rav.

Prior to the war, Rav Jacobson, as chairman of Agudath Israel's Keren HaTorah, had travelled extensively and met many people throughout the Jewish world. Now he used his experiences to break the ice with the girls. "Oh," he would say, "So you are so-and-so's daughter... I knew your father before the war. And you," he would smile, turning to another girl, "Are related to so-and-so... I remember the family well from Warsaw (or Cracow... or Budapest...)." After years of isolation, here was someone who knew who they were, from where they had come, who their parents had been. They loved it, and it was the first step in helping them open up and talk.

But this was only the beginning.

Becoming a Family

The initial period, understandably enough, was one of adjustment.

The only activity in which the girls had any real interest at that time was trying to find out if any of their relatives had survived the war.

Even after they arrived in Lidingo, some would merely sit and stare off into space for hours at a time, while others simply refused to leave the safety of their beds, day and night. For them, life and its realities were dull and meaningless.

Another problem proved to be the diversity of the girls' backgrounds.

They came from Poland, Transylvania, Galicia, Hungary, Slovakia, Yugoslavia, and more. The differences in origins and custom bred a certain alienation. The Polish girls were convinced that they were the most intelligent of the group; the Hungarians felt that they were the best educated; while the Galicians and Slovakians maintained that it was actually they who were the smartest.

At first, Rebbetzin Jacobson had hoped that with time, the girls would overcome their differences, and understand that one's country of origin was really of no great significance. When she saw that the girls persisted in their divisiveness, she decided that the time had come to take the bull by the horns. One morning after breakfast, she stood up and asked the girls to remain seated.

"Girls," she began, "There's something I would like you all to think about." She chose her words carefully, so that no one would be offended. They were all still so sensitive! "Do you know what a wonderful opportunity has fallen into your laps?" she said, including them all in her loving smile. "Our group has come here from all over Europe. What a tremendous opportunity for us all to learn one from one another!"

Their interest was piqued, and they waited for the Rebbetzin to explain.

"Just think: the Polish girls can learn enthusiasm and order from the Hungarians. The Hungarians can learn from the Polish girls' greater life experience. We can all learn diligence from the Lithuanians.

Everyone's homeland excels in some special way, and we can gain from each other's unique talents, right here in our own home!"

The Rebbetzin's words came straight from a heart overflowing with love and compassion, and the girls accepted and absorbed the message.

Slowly, gradually, they came to appreciate their companions' better qualities, and made an effort to learn from them. In so doing, they became a united family: the Lidingo family.

Ever sensitive to the girls' emotional needs, Rav Jacobson found his own way of dealing with the problem of their diverse backgrounds. Some of the girls at Lidingo came from Chassidic homes, and wanted to maintain their family traditions. Rav Jacobson understood and encouraged them. One day, he made an unusual announcement.

"Girls, I know that some of you are from Chassidic families. While I personally am not Chassidic, far be it from me to distance you from your sainted parents' way of life; all of Judaism is sacred. I have with me a book about the Baal Shem Tov and his disciples. Every week, I'd like another girl to read a chapter of the book and prepare a talk about one of the *rabbanim*. It will be an excellent way for us all to learn together about how these righteous men lived their lives, and how we can improve our own service of G-d."

The talks delivered by the girls became a regular *Shabbos* feature in Lidingo. They also served as a subtle vehicle to teach them that the Jewish people, themselves included, no matter how far-flung, are in reality one family.

Another early source of dissension was the question of language. Each girl in Lidingo knew two languages: her native tongue, and German.

Understandably, the very sound of German disgusted them, and it was out of the question for it be spoken in school. After careful deliberation, the staff decided that the common tongue would be Hebrew. Many of the girls had some familiarity with Hebrew from pre-war prayers, synagogue attendance, and religious studies. In addition, the staff hoped to eventually bring all the girls to *Eretz Yisrael*, where Hebrew was spoken, so the introduction of the language would be of practical benefit as well.

With time, the girls were finally able to give up their suspicions and lower their defenses, and they began to tell their stories. Their accounts were tragic in their similarity: soul-numbing degradation, agonizing hunger, painful beatings, endless hours spent standing on tired, swollen feet in bitter cold and scorching heat. Again, Rav Jacobson's care and empathy helped them overcome this hurdle on the road to recovery.

* * *

The *Yamim Noraim* came and went, and the Swedish winter was beginning to make its presence felt. A few hardy flowers still decorated the lawn, but they were buffetted by cold winds and rain. By now, however, even the grayest of clouds was unable to put a damper on the spirits of the girls who had come to love Lidingo, where for the first time in years, they could finally feel at home. It was the perfect time to introduce an orderly teaching program.

The School

Chaya Markusewitsch, a graduate of the Hebrew Gymnasium in Lithuania and a certified Hebrew teacher, now a young widow, and Ahuva, whose studies at the Gymnasium had been interrupted by the war but whose Hebrew was excellent nonetheless, were the first teachers in Lidingo.

They began their teaching assignments with not a little apprehension, tempered by a great deal of hope.

The girls, on the other hand, were delighted. Deprived of any sort of formal education for years, their spiritual and intellectual thirst turned the girls of Lidingo into exemplary students. Even those girls who were less than studious by nature now exerted themselves to the utmost, suddenly eager to learn. Anxious to divert the girls' minds from the grim brooding over the past which had occupied them almost exclusively until then, Rav and Rebbetzin Jacobson carefully designed an intensive educational program which would keep them stimulated and busy. There was a full, well-rounded curriculum including geography, mathematics, biology, arts and crafts, painting, and more. There was also a wide-ranging program of Jewish studies. The Rebbetzin, as she was called, gave highly popular classes in Jewish thought and *Tanach*, which none of the girls would dream of missing. Mr. Nissan Igell taught English.

Eventually, the school grew into three classes. The very first group of girls formed Class One, which earned a sterling reputation during their three years in

Lidingo. Those who came later, after more extended hospital stays, were Class Two, while the most recent arrivals made up Class Three. But once again, the beginning was not easy.

Chaya and Ahuvah quickly realized that nothing about their new pupils was ordinary: neither their wildly divergent backgrounds, their ages and academic standing, nor their horrifying past, the memory of which never left them. They were way below age level academically and even more so in their knowledge of Judaism. Even those who had come from extremely religious families had been torn away from them before they could fully absorb the piety of their late parents and the spiritual environment of their homes. Their knowledge of Torah was minimal; most of it had been forgotten in the camps, leaving them with only a few vague, tattered memories.

Perhaps worst of all was the situation of the Polish girls: their ignorance was compounded by attitudes grossly antithetical to Torah Judaism. Even before the war, many young Jews in Poland had been influenced by alien ideas and drifted away from Torah. Some gave up their observances altogether, while others, out of respect for their parents, had still maintained a facade. For the girls who been through the camps, the trauma of their horrifying experiences during the war had almost obliterated any remaining vestiges of their faith.

And they were not the only ones. All the girls who came to Lidingo, young as they were, had suffered terribly, and most had lost their entire families. Gnawing doubts about the fundamentals of Judaism left them empty and miserable. They had groped desperately for some sort of understanding of the terrible destruction they had witnessed, but there had been no one to guide them. Bitterness, despair, and rebellion filled their aching, broken hearts. Even had they wanted to find solace in prayer, they had forgotten the *alef-bais*.

The first step, then, was to begin with the prayer book. As the girls learned, word by word, to read our age-old *siddur*, it seemed that the very grass on which they sat with their teachers lifted its head to listen. As the words began to come more easily to their lips, the angels in heaven must have carried the glad tidings to their martyred parents: the eternal chain had not been broken after all.

From *siddur* they went on to *Chumash*. The girls invested a great deal of effort in this subject, despite the fact that they had no textbooks, only the notebooks over which they pored for hours in the afternoons.

Singly and in pairs, with the stronger students cheerfully helping the weaker ones, they studied and reviewed, their ever-present sadness forgotten for the moment. These studies led to a determination to work on their *middos*, the character traits which make up each individual's personality. After years of raw struggle for survival, they were able now find both the time and the need to work on improving their relationships with those around them.

One of the girls remembers her schooling in Lidingo:

"Generally speaking, we were quite industrious; we didn't want to waste time. A cancelled class was viewed as a loss. Even the poorer students were influenced by the prevailing positive attitude towards study and self-improvement.

"Eventually, we decided to attempt additional independent study, beginning with *Navi* and some of the classical *mussar* works. The few texts we had were passed from hand to hand. Since we wanted not only to understand what we were learning, but also to commit some of the material to memory, we became quite fluent in sections of *Mesillas Yesharim*.

"The Rebbetzin's classes in *Chumash, Tehillim,* and *Navi Yeshaya* had an enormous impact on us. While she taught one class, the others had secular studies. Often, girls would sneak out of math or biology or whatever else they were doing and stand outside the window to listen in on the Rebbetzin's classes. The girls would juggle their chore assignments so that they wouldn't have to miss Torah classes.

"Some afternoons, we would sit together, peeling vegetables for the kitchen. At times like this, we would form a circle. One girl would either read aloud or else recite from the material we were studying, and the others would listen. Not only did sessions like these improve our grades, they gave us a precious sense of closeness and friendship."

* * *

The policy of the Rav and Rebbetzin was not to criticize the girls for unsuitable behavior. There were no rules about what was permitted and what was forbidden. They taught by personal example. The Rebbetzin was a born educator, whose own behavior provided a subtle but powerful message.

From time to time, guest lecturers would come to Lidingo. Sometimes the Rebbetzin would amplify upon the lecturer's talk, while in other instances she said nothing. On one occasion, a speaker delivered an impassioned talk about *Eretz Yisrael.* He taught the girls a song which included the following stanza:

It's two thousand years since our wanderings began,
And we have suffered enough!

This was one of the rare occasions when the Rebbetzin intervened. The girls recognized the telltale red spots on her neck, which appeared whenever she was upset. She chose her words carefully.

"It is very difficult for me to stand in front of you girls, the very ones who have suffered so greatly, and tell you that it is forbidden for us to set limits, to give advice to the Holy One, blessed be He, and to say that we have already suffered enough." Her voice broke; it was obvious that it required enormous effort on her part to speak this way. "Who am I, who did not share your agony, to dare to say you have not `suffered enough'?" she said in a quavering voice. "Yet despite everything, this is something we as Jews cannot say. Our comprehension is limited and we are not the ones to keep accounts. We can only have faith and complete trust in G-d's wisdom."

The girls were quiet, but they understood - and agreed. They had learned much from the Rebbetzin, enough to enable them to absorb even this poignant lesson. Their years in Lidingo would continue to provide them with a Torah legacy that would remain with them not only in their own lifetimes, but for generations to come.

* * *

Much of Lidingo's success, both as a school and as a home, was the result of its carefully cultivated atmosphere. There was no coercion; the girls were not compelled to do anything. Never did the Rebbetzin impose her opinion or sermonize. She taught, and the girls, in their own way and on their own level, drew their own conclusions. There was never any direct criticism. If rebuke was called for, the Rebbetzin wisely wove it into her discussions of *Chumash* or *Navi*, rather than confront the girls directly, and they understood and responded accordingly. They knew that their teachers loved them and wanted only the best for them, a realization which sweetened study, chores, and even an occasional - albeit indirect - reprimand.

Raizy

The bright, moon full summer shone through the window, right into Raizy's eyes. She tossed. She turned. She pulled the blanket over her head, then buried her face under the pillow, but it was all to no avail. The sleep, she so desperately needed to heal her tired body and equally tired soul, evaded her. Eventually, Raizy decided to move her pillow to the foot of the bed, thus avoiding the glare of the moonlight, but still she could not sleep.

"Raizy," her mother had once told her when she was a little girl, "If you can't fall asleep, just lie down with your eyes closed and count, as many numbers as you know. Just keep counting, and before you know it, you'll be asleep."

Why not? Raizy began to count: One, two, three... what next? Somehow the numbers had blurred into a confused jumble in her mind; she just couldn't remember what came next. How embarrassing! Even Avrumi, her little brother, knew how to count. Avrumi... How old had he been when she had seen him last? Three? Or had he already turned four? Through a painful haze, Raizy could picture him as he had been before the war: bright and alert, with happy, laughing eyes, his *peyos* swinging wildly as he ran through the fields near their home.

Where was he now? Had they killed him too? Or maybe... Nonsense, Raizy told herself. Of course they killed him. What use could a child like him have been to the Nazis? Sleep forgotten, her mind continued to wander, taking its usual nightly route...

Even if she had to admit that Avrumi was probably gone, what about the others? Where were Rocheleh and Chanke and Dinush? Couldn't they still be alive somewhere? Perhaps she would yet find them someday.

And Shloimy. The last time she had seen him was on the train after the roundup. He had waved goodbye and shouted to her over the din, "Take care of Mamma and the little ones. We'll all pray for them..."

After that she couldn't hear any more. The train began to move, taking her beloved brother away forever. Much later, she learned that he had tried - unsuccessfully - to escape from the concentration camp where he was imprisoned, and died climbing over an electrified fence. Shloimy... At the age of fourteen, he had returned his holy soul to his Creator.

And what had become of Dudi? Mr. Finkel, their old neighbor, had told her that he had seen Dudi in a men's labor camp. He had lied to the camp commandant, telling him that he was a skilled metalworker. Without batting an eyelash, he had proved his claim, miraculously turning a piece of metal into a work of art under the commandant's critical eye. Since then, Mr. Finkel told her, he had used his comparatively advantageous position to help others, despite his own long hours of hard physical labor. Never had he lost his faith in the One Above, no matter what. When faced with the ultimate test, Raizy mused, our pampered Dudi, the dreamer, the one we always laughed at for having his head in the clouds, had shown inner strength and determination we never knew he was capable of.

Raizy shifted uneasily in her bed. Enough of this, she told herself, enough! I want to sleep. I want to stretch out in a comfortable bed like this one, with clean sheets, and sleep as long as I like. Not standing up, not sitting cramped against a mass of other girls the way we did in the camps - lying down, like a civilized human being. The girls around her were sleeping peacefully, but try as she might, Raizy simply could not fall asleep. She tried counting again, but the unbidden memories and speculations continued to torment her. It was nearly morning when she finally dozed off. All too soon, the usual early morning noises intruded on her long awaited rest.

"Leave me alone," she mumbled, "I want to sleep. I'm so tired... can't you let me sleep?"

But the voices of the bickering girls rose even louder. "Look at you, taking all the water for yourself. Can't you leave a little for somebody else? How selfish can you get?"

That did it. "Look who's talking!" came the angry retort, "You ate five whole slices of bread yesterday! Were you thinking about anybody else then?" "You're just jealous!" "Jealous? Of you? Don't make me laugh!"

"Enough already!" Raizy begged, "Can't you let me sleep just a little longer? Stop shouting!"

"Sure, go ahead and sleep. It's your funeral," one of the girls said bitterly, "Then when there's no water left for you, don't expect anybody to give you hers. Haven't you learned yet that water has to be guarded?"

"I'll have you know that I've been up since five this morning guarding my water - not that it's any of your business," another girl chimed in.

"What's the matter with you people? Can't you see that there's no shortage of water here? Do me a favor: take mine, and just let me sleep!" Raizy pleaded.

The angry shouting gave way to quiet grumbling. Everyone was awake now, yawning and rubbing their eyes. A new day had begun in Lidingo. Who knew what it would bring?

Raizy sat up in bed, watching her roommates: young girls who had grown up before their time, and teenage girls who were already old. What they all had in common was an abiding distrust for those around them, the legacy of a cruel war for survival. She listened carelessly as they talked, her eyes on the window above her bed. No, the moon wasn't there anymore. She might as well get up.

"*Yadan, dve, tchi, tchistari* (one, two, three, four)," she mumbled as she headed for the faucet for *netilas yadayim*. So she did remember! She must have been confused last night.

What was that business about five slices of bread that the girls were fighting about? she wondered drowsily. They always warn us not to stuff ourselves... five slices at one meal? It was true that the portions of food were carefully measured in Lidingo's dining room: not too much at a time, but certainly not too little. There was plenty of food at mealtimes, but for the girls' own good, their intake still had to be carefully monitored. Their shrunken, abused systems had to adjust slowly to normal food, and the girls had to relearn normal eating habits. Just look at Mashie, the new girl who came yesterday, Raizy thought. I've never seen anyone so thin! All in all, the girls here were definitely full of surprises, she decided.

"What a dreamer," said a voice from behind her, "Haven't you woken up yet?"

Raizy picked up the washcup and studied it carefully. I wonder if the girls could really be right, she thought nervously. Maybe there really is a shortage of water here. Maybe it really would be better to hurry. She suddenly noticed that she was the only one left in the room. "One thing is certain," she said aloud, "I can't fill my stomach with dreams." She hurried down to the dining room.

A smiling, white-jacketed woman went from table to table, asking, "Is everything all right? Does everyone have enough food? How did you all sleep last night?" She received a barrage of replies, mostly positive. Pleased, she moved on to the next table, still smiling.

Raizy downed her oatmeal in record time, keeping a careful eye on the smiling woman all the while. Raizy's skirt had a big pocket. As soon as the woman moved on to the next table, she planned to hide a slice of bread in it. Why take chances? Besides, perhaps she could share it with the new girl, Mashie. Who knew how long it had been since the poor thing had eaten her fill?

* * *

Raizy remembered the night she had arrived in Lidingo... Even in the pale moonlight, she could see that the building was old and neglected, surrounded by thick, overgrown weeds. Slowly, hesitantly, she and her friends knocked timidly at the rather shabby front door.

So this was Lidingo. Here, they had been told, in this place with the unpronounceable name, they would be happy. They would have a new family, a Jewish atmosphere, and the chance to resume their studies. It had been so long since any of them had actually gone to school!

As they lingered at the doorstep, Raizy could hear voices from inside. Probably the girls who arrived two weeks ago from Poland, she thought absently. I wonder what they're like?

Sorke finally mustered enough courage to ring the bell. A short woman promptly appeared in answer to the ring. She had friendly eyes and a warm, motherly smile.

"*Shalom*, welcome," she said in Yiddish, "Please, come right in."

Raizy's pleasure at the friendly greeting was marred by her ever present fear of the unknown. She clung tightly to the precious bag containing her two blouses, a skirt, and several other small items. These things were hers, and she intended to guard them carefully. I won't give them up, she thought fiercely, never! They're mine!

But the woman didn't ask her to surrender her bag. She merely offered them refreshments, after which, she said, she would show them to their room. Raizy accepted a drink, but was too nervous to eat.

"Here you are, girls," said the woman cheerfully, ushering them into a large room. "You can each choose whichever bed you like, and a shelf in the closet. I'll bring you sheets and towels in a minute," she added with another smile. She set off for the linen closet, leaving them alone in the room.

Raizy looked at the obviously new wallpaper, at the gleaming windows, and at the crisply ironed curtains. Everything was sparkling clean. She went over to one of the beds and poked gingerly at the straw mattress, sparking a lively argument over who would get which bed. Before they reached a decision, however, the Polish girls, by now old-timers in Lidingo, arrived to welcome the newcomers.

"Has Mrs. Igell given you sheets yet?" asked a girl named Malinka. Raizy made a mental note of the name - the woman who had greeted them was called Mrs. Igell. However, she didn't care for Malinka's manner and didn't bother answering her. Who had asked her to interfere? Couldn't she see that they still did not have sheets?

"Look," pointed out one of the Polish girls, "The mattresses are made of straw, but they're comfortable. Anyway, you get so tired here that you sleep well at night no matter what kind of mattress you have."

Aha! thought Raizy bitterly, I knew it! It's the same story all over again: another rotten labor camp. And I thought my troubles were over, fool that I am. It's a good thing I didn't give them my bag; I've got two slices of bread in there. I guess we'll just have to learn the ropes and get ourselves properly `organized' here. It looks like the nightmare isn't over yet.

Yet as she looked around her, she was somehow not so sure. Why did the girls look so happy? Why had this Mrs. Igell, as they called her, been so friendly? Could she be making a mistake?

Mrs. Igell reappeared, her gentle face still adorned with that same good-natured smile. "I've got sheets here for everyone, and towels and soap. If anyone needs something - a comb, a toothbrush, or anything else - let me know, and I'll take care of it right away. Is there anything else I can do for you now?"

When no one answered, she said, "Then I'll leave you to get settled. I'm sure the other girls will be happy to assist you, their newly arrived sisters in our Lidingo family."

Raizy could not explain why she already liked this woman whom she had just barely met, but whose presence generated a safe, soothing ambience. Even if her suspicions were correct and this really was a labor camp, if Mrs. Igell was in charge, it couldn't be that bad.

Raizy still had to choose a bed, no easy task. She did not want the bed next to the window, because of the glare of the moonlight. On the other hand, if she'd ever have to escape at night, the bed near the window would really be best. In the end, it was Tzilka who made the choice for her, by choosing the bed near the window for herself. Raizy assumed that Tzilka was also worried about the need for a sudden escape; one could never be too careful. Raizy took the third bed to the right of the door. After making it up, she added Mrs. Igell's soap and towel to her private hoard and placed her bag at the head of the bed, carefully hidden under the pillow. She couldn't risk putting her few possessions in the closet. These things were hers, and who knew what the morrow would bring?

The other newcomers worked quietly alongside her, making up their own beds. They could hear loud voices from the next room, speaking Polish. Raizy had heard enough stories in the camps about treacherous Poles to know she would have to be careful, living in close quarters with them. Poor Raizy - little did she know that all those horror stories were but another vicious trick of the Nazis to turn the unfortunate Jews against one another, eliminating the chances of a united revolt.

In the relative safety of their own beds in the darkened room, the girls conversed in furtive whispers, planning for a quick escape in case it should become necessary. They had not gotten very far when the lights were switched on and Mrs. Igell stepped into the room.

"My girls," she said gently, "I've come to wish you all a good night. I didn't expect you to turn off the light so early." She went from bed to bed, spending a few private minutes with each of them, asking them their names and where they were from, stroking their hair, trying to make them feel comfortable and welcome. After she had spoken to them all, she said aloud, "My husband and I live on the ground floor of the building. He is the administrator of the school. Don't ever hesitate to come to us if there's any problem. He's learning Torah right now, but you'll meet him tomorrow."

Raizy was somewhat reassured. Mrs. Igell said her husband was learning Torah. They certainly didn't sound like Nazis. Perhaps they really were Jews, after all?

"What time do we get up here?" she suddenly blurted out.

"At six," said Mrs. Igell. "Is there anything else I can do for you?" There was no response. "Good night to you all then, and sleep well!" Alone again, the girls were quiet, absorbed in their own thoughts. Raizy tried to make plans for the next day. A six o'clock wake-up indicated a tightly run labor camp, she decided. There would probably be work assignments and a recitation of camp regulations first thing in the morning. Raizy made a bold decision: she would not get up at six, even if she was really awake. She would pretend to be asleep, just to see what they would do to her. More than anything else, that would tell her just what sort of place this was. If they were going to kill her, then so be it. She would rather get it over with immediately. Not only would it end her own suffering, it would alert her friends to the true nature of this latest camp.

Even though it seemed to Raizy that she had just fallen asleep, the clock read a quarter to six. She must have slept for several hours. What a luxury... she snuggled comfortably under her blanket. Suddenly, she was seized with uncontrollable trembling. She distinctly heard a voice from downstairs, and it was speaking German! There was no mistaking the despised language in which she had taken orders for so long. She listened closely, trying to make out what was being said. She could hear now that it was a woman's voice. She shuddered. The female SS guards had often been even worse than the men.

She squeezed her eyes shut. I'm asleep, asleep! she told herself frantically. She thought of the escape plan she had worked out last night: now was the time. For the briefest moment, she was tempted to stay where she was, rather than risk being shot by the guards, but decided against it. What was the use? She would take her chances.

But it was too late. The German woman was coming closer and closer now, announcing that it was time to get up. Raizy could hear the Polish girls getting out of bed, and felt a surge of anger. Those hypocrites, she thought, I knew it all along! Couldn't they have warned us last night? Then we still had a chance to get away, but now it's too late.

She burrowed more deeply under the blanket.

"Boy, can that one sleep," she heard Miraleh say, "The noise doesn't bother her at all."

If only she knew!

"Girls," someone called, "Hurry up, the Rebbetzin is waiting downstairs."

Her roommates hustled along obediently, and Raizy was left alone. She smiled sadly at her friends' foolish innocence. Rebbetzin indeed - that's what they said. It was brilliant! Call an SS guard a Rebbetzin, and they all believe it and fall right into the trap. But not Raizy, she was smarter than that.

She lay quietly in bed, not moving a muscle, waiting for something to happen and wondering why it was so quiet. No one came to wake her. Maybe they forgot about me, she thought. This could be the perfect opportunity to escape. But still she hesitated. What if it wasn't a labor camp? Maybe it would be better to wait.

She heard the sound of footsteps in the corridor, and her muscles tensed: they were coming to get her. Had she made a mistake? Should she have escaped while she'd still had the chance? Should she have gone down with the others? I'll close my eyes tight, she told herself, and I won't move. Who is it? The SS woman?

she thought desperately. She allowed one eye to flutter open for the barest fraction of a second. Through the tiny crack she saw Mrs. Igell.

The problem was that Mrs. Igell saw her too.

"You must be tired this morning, Raizy," she said, "Feel free to sleep late today if you like. It's alright. The other girls are outside on the grass. You can join them there when you get up, but first come down to the dining room and have something to eat. I'll be downstairs," she said, closing the door quietly behind her.

And that was all. She didn't berate her for breaking the rules, and she didn't punish her. As for the other girls, they were on the grass. Or so she said. Couldn't she be lying? Maybe it was part of the plot!

Raizy stayed in bed for another half an hour, her mind racing. Should she get up, or would it be safer to stay in bed? "Be brave, Raizy," she whispered softly to herself, "You can't stay in bed forever. Get up and get it over with." Summoning all her courage, she decided to confront the German woman, face-to-face.

Maybe she had only dreamed that she'd heard German?

In her heart of hearts, Raizy had to admit that Lidingo neither looked nor sounded like a labor camp, but experience had taught her to be careful.

Before she could change her mind, she quickly washed her hands and face, dressed, and went downstairs. If she was going to see the true face of the camp, it might as well be now.

She was still on the staircase when she heard the voice again. A woman's voice, speaking German. She tried to make out the words, but the pounding of her heart was louder than any voice could be. She tiptoed silently down the stairs and put her ear to the door of Mrs. Igell's apartment. It was just as she had suspected: the voice was coming from inside the apartment!

So this was it: the deception was over. There was an SS officer inside that apartment, chatting comfortably with Mrs. Igell - a Nazi after all, despite her pretty words. Raizy pressed her ear closer to the door, trying to overhear the conversation, but she couldn't understand what they were saying. The Voice came closer. There was no time to run before the door opened, revealing a woman in a turban, long dress, and black shoes. The woman stopped short, dumbfounded.

"Can I help you?" she asked in German.

Raizy heard and understood, but was too petrified to speak. Her eyes rolled wildly, searching for an avenue of escape.

"Don't be afraid," the woman said in German, "Here, you can come in."

Sure, thought Raizy, by now near hysteria, don't be afraid - absolutely nothing to worry about. Just come right in!

To her own surprise, she found herself walking into the apartment. Why couldn't she bring herself to turn around and run? Absurdly, Mrs. Igell was sitting on the couch, folding laundry.

"Oh, Raizy, good morning!" she said cheerfully, "You must be hungry. Come and join us for breakfast. We haven't eaten yet either."

Watch it, Raizy, watch it, she's two-faced, said Raizy's mind. But her heart suspected otherwise. She approached the two women, still unable to speak.

"What's the matter with the girl?" the tall woman asked in German. "She must be exhausted, whether from the camps or from quarantine. She may still be frightened and suspicious. She'll join us for breakfast, alright?"

"Of course," the woman replied in German. She tried to stroke Raizy's head. Raizy began to tremble.

"Don't touch me!" she burst out hysterically. "You two-faced hypocrite! How could you say that you're

Jews? Go ahead, go ahead and kill me, send me to the gas chambers!" Raizy screamed uncontrollably. Her breathing was harsh and labored, and her chest rose and fell. Her hands and feet shook. The two women looked at the terrified girl. For a moment, they were silent.

"Now I understand," murmured Mrs. Igell, "You poor girl. Raizy," she said aloud, speaking in Yiddish, "I want you to sit down and listen to me. This is Rebbetzin Jacobson. She was born in Germany. That's why she speaks German. She lived in Denmark, and from there, together with her husband and many other Jews, she was admitted to Sweden by the Swedish authorities, just as you and your friends were now. She and Rav Jacobson started this home for Jewish girls like you. I'll introduce you to the Rav and you'll see for yourself that everything is alright. They are here to help you. German is their mother tongue, and the only one in which they can communicate with the girls. I understand your fears, but you're safe now. Raizy, please believe me. There's nothing to be afraid of anymore."

Mrs. Igell spoke calmly and quietly. Raizy listened, her eyes darting back and forth. Her breathing slowly returned to normal. As Mrs. Igell spoke, the Rebbetzin smiled and nodded her agreement, at a loss for words in her distress over the incident.

Raizy bowed her head and gave vent to her emotions in a torrent of tears. Mrs. Igell embraced her and stroked her hair. "You can cry, my child, cry as much as you want. But with G-d's help, you'll never have to cry again."

Brachie and Bayle

In May, 1945, shortly before the end of the war, Count Folke Bernadotte, a Swedish aristocrat, went to Germany on behalf of the Swedish Red Cross to rescue inmates of the death camps. The Nazis were willing to negotiate an exchange of Swedish citizens in Nazi occupied territories for German prisoners of war. When the supply of Swedish citizens was exhausted, they were willing to release some lucky Jews as well.

Sick and starved, these Jews began to arrive in Sweden, where they were immediately given emergency medical treatment by devoted physicians and nurses. There were over ten thousand of them, from both religious and secular families. The majority of the refugees were women from Poland, Hungary, Czechoslovakia, and Lithuania. Some had endured as many as six years of torture in the camps, and were broken in spirit as well as in body. The Swedish branch of the Vaad HaHatzalah, affiliated with the Agudath Harabbanim of America, did their utmost to provide them with urgently needed relief. They soon found out that many of the women longed for *Shabbos* candles and prayer books, while the men needed *tallis* and *tefillin*.

Fortunately, Adolph Gustav VI, at that time still crown prince of Sweden, had a profound appreciation of the Jewish religion and was especially sensitive to the situation of the observant Jews. This noble man's understanding of their needs and wishes led him to establish special camps for orthodox refugees. Another

Swedish aristocrat who distinguished himself in his efforts for the Jewish people is Raoul Wallenberg, who saved thousands of Jews at the risk of his own life. These Righteous Gentiles have earned a place in the World to Come, and will forever be remebered by grateful Jewish people.

* * *

However, not everyone was quite so helpful to the Jewish refugees in Sweden. For reasons of their own, Stockholm's Reform community, leaders and congregation, sought to estrange them from Torah by telling them that traditional Judaism was dead, replaced by a new, progressive version. They went so far as to encourage intermarriage with non-Jews. Typical of this attitude was the talk delivered by the congregation's chief cantor, (not to be confused with the assistant cantor, Mr. Bernstein) who came on behalf of the rabbi, Dr. Ehrenpreis, to visit Varnamo, a camp populated mostly by Czechoslovakian refugees.

"Girls," he said, "I hear that a number of you refuse to eat the meat served here, because you say that it is not kosher." Several heads nodded in agreement. At last, someone was willing to take them seriously!

"Then I want you all to listen carefully," he said, slowly and emphatically, "Forget all that nonsense. The Judaism you remember is gone forever. It's old fashioned and obsolete, and it doesn't exist any more. As a rabbi (!), I tell you that you may eat any kind of meat you like without the slightest hesitation." He smiled triumphantly as he observed the girls' wide open eyes.

Non-kosher meat? How could anyone say it was permissible to eat non-kosher meat? Their lives in a religious framework were light-years behind them, but this was too much.

Some of the braver ones dared to question the "rabbi." "How can *treife* meat be kosher?" they asked. "Everyone knows Jews have special laws about kosher slaughter."

"Come now," replied the cantor, "Don't you realize that there are simply no longer any *shochtim*? You saw for yourselves that they were all killed by the Nazis." He scanned their troubled faces and smiled confidently. "But it's really no problem. There is no shortage of meat in Sweden."

The girls conferred quietly among themselves. They were terribly confused. They had never heard of a situation where there were no *shochtim* and everyone ate non-kosher meat. At home, they had always learned that for centuries, Jews had made countless sacrifices to keep the Torah's commandments, including the one to eat only kosher food. As for the rabbi, he looked very different from those they remembered from home. But then, wasn't everything different now? Maybe this rabbi was right. Had they not seen with their own eyes how untold numbers of pious Jews were burned, hung, gassed, and shot? Perhaps they really all were gone.

"Is the *rav* saying that there are no more *shochtim*?" asked one of the girls. He nodded.

"Why can't some of the men here learn the laws of *shechitah*?" asked another.

From the "rabbi's" quick response, it seemed that this was precisely the question he had been waiting for. "Because there are very few surviving Jewish men," he said smoothly. "Certainly not enough to rebuild the old world from scratch. But you, my dear girls, are young. You have your whole lives ahead of you. Join us and we will help you. You can all build new lives, married to fine young Swedish men. Forget the past, be happy, and you need never again be persecuted as Jews."

Among the girls seated in the hall were two sisters named Brachie and Bayle. They had arrived in Varnamo just a week ago from quarantine in Landskrona. They found themselves unable to believe the words of the man who presented himself as a rabbi. They remembered the *rav* of their pre-war community, a pious, scholarly Jew, the antithesis of this person who was encouraging them to eat *treife* meat and marry non-Jews. In fact, their own uncle was a *rav*, and he also was nothing like this so-called Swedish rabbi. But then, perhaps their understanding of things belonged to a past that was dead and buried; maybe things really were different now.

Compounding their confusion was the fact that the "rabbi" - actually a Reform cantor - was singing *Kol Nidrei!* The melody was beautiful and the rendition impressive, but *Kol Nidrei?* Now?

Brachie and Bayle decided that their best bet was to write to their uncle in *Eretz Yisrael*, Rav Dushinsky. They would tell him what was happening and ask his opinion. Rav Dushinsky, leader of Jerusalem's *Aida Hachareidis*, assessed the situation immediately and contacted Rav Jacobson. Rav Jacobson got in touch with the girls at once and invited them to come to Lidingo. They were joined by several others who hesitated to accept the arguments of the Swedish "rabbi."

Unfortunately, however, Bayle, Brachie, and their friends were exceptional. Most of the girls, traumatized by the suffering they had endured and vulnerable without their lost families, were taken in, and unwittingly resigned themselves to a life far removed from traditional Judaism.

When the girls arrived in Lidingo shortly before *Rosh Hashanah*, the Polish girls were already in residence. They supressed their mutual suspicion and distrust; there was too much to do to prepare for the upcoming holiday. On their second day in Lidingo, the newcomers joined the girls in cleaning the dormitory and immersing new dishes in the *mikveh*. Brachie and Bayle were too happy for words. Here, no one would tell them to eat non-kosher meat because there were no more *shochtim*! And here, the *rav* was like the one they remembered from home.

* * *

The suffering they had known in Auschwitz, the endless hours on their feet waiting for their numbers to be called in the burning heat of summer and the freezing cold of winter, the sleepless nights cramped on crowded bunks like so many sardines, had not been enough to make Brachie and Bayle forget their cherished memories of the world they had lost. Nor had the horrific sights they had witnessed daily: the frozen bodies stacked casually along the camps' narrow paths, and the deadly roll calls. Under the watchful eye of Dr. Mengele, they had seen the sick calmly consigned to the crematoria while the others shivered, not knowing when their turn would come. For Brachie and Bayle, the next stop had been Bergen-Belsen, where death took its toll by means of starvation, disease, and filth. They had watched in horror as people collapsed on the camp's streets, too starved and exhausted to go on living.

It was difficult to understand how these two frail young girls had managed to survive despite it all. The Nazis, undeterred by the inmates' pathetic physical condition, had squeezed every last ounce of strength out of them. They were sent to clear the rubble from the German city of Braunschweig (Brunswick) after the Allied bombing. In the freezing, snowy cold of the German winter nights, dressed only in thin summer clothes, they would return to their quarters in a stable to sleep on the wet straw, soaked by the melting snow.

* * *

One morning shortly after their arrival in Lidingo, Bayle shook her sister awake, obviously quite agitated. "Brachie," she whispered, "We've got to find that room. We have to tell everyone."

"What?" mumbled Brachie, still only half awake, "Which room? Where? Can it wait a minute until I wash my hands?" She washed her hands and face and, now wide awake and curious, turned to look at her sister.

Jewish property that was confiscated by the Nazis

"What's this all about, Bayle?" she asked.

A broad smile covered Bayle's face. "Do you remember Bendorf, the factory where we assembled airplane parts for the Germans?"

"Sure," replied Brachie. She still did not understand what her sister was getting at. "What about it?"

Bayle explained. "You didn't work with me there. You were up on the second floor, but I worked downstairs, in the production rooms below ground level. The factory was built on a salt mine 300 feet underground."

"I never heard that," said Brachie, surprised, "Who told you?"

"One of the soldiers. We were in the elevator on the way down. I made some comment about how modern the factory was, and he took it as a compliment. He explained very proudly that the huge halls where we worked were carved out of the salt."

"And that's what you want to find? What on earth for?" "Don't be ridiculous. Who cares about a salt mine? But listen to this. One day, when the guard was in an especially good mood, I complained that it had been months since we'd seen the light of day. You know what he answered? `There are things here which are much more interesting than daylight. Come with me and I'll show you what I mean.' He took me into a big room which none of us girls had ever seen. It was crammed with magnificent oil paintings, crystal, and solid gold vases. I couldn't believe my eyes. I'd never seen so many beautiful and obviously valuable things... all stolen from Jewish homes. He told me that this was Goebbel's treasure room. `You can tell the angels about it,' he said.

"I understood that he'd only shown me the room because none of us were going to leave there alive. When I thought about where all those treasures came from, I was furious. I wanted to find a way to get back into that room and destroy every last item in there."

"And?" asked Brachie, fascinated.

"He never took me back there. Then, when Count Bernadotte came to the camp and we were all so confused and drained, not knowing if we would ever really be released, I just forgot about it. But if we could find it now, maybe we could return the valuables to their owners..." her voice trailed off. She looked pleadingly at Brachie. Just don't say no, her eyes begged.

Brachie had been entirely caught up in her sister's torrent of words. It was only now that she noticed that several of their roommates were sitting up in their beds, listening eagerly.

She inched over to Bayle. "Listen to me, Bayle," she said quietly. Bayle moved a little closer to Brachie, who said, "It's not quite as simple as you make it sound - as if all we have to do is go back to Braunschweig, open the door to Goebbel's vault, and give everything back. For one thing, Germany was bombed by the Allies during the war. Who knows if anything is left of the underground factory? And even if it is still there, do you think you're the only one who knew about the vault? There must have been others who knew, and emptied it before the Allies came. Besides, are you really so sure that what you saw was Goebbel's personal cache? Couldn't that soldier have been lying, or have made a mistake? Maybe he was joking, or just showing off."

Bayle was clearly disappointed. "Do you really think it's impossible? Couldn't it still be worth a try? If you had seen that room, you'd also want to go back and look for it."

"No, Bayle," said Brachie gently, but firmly. "Just forget the whole thing. Leave that treasure for someone else to worry about it, if it still exists, and concentrate on the real treasure G-d has given us: our new life here with the Lidingo family. Be honest. In your wildest dreams, could you ever have pictured anything so precious?"

Bayle's brilliant smile was all the answer Brachie needed. She looked around at her roommates who, curious as they were, had stayed out of the conversation, and was enveloped by a wave of warmth. They were all her sisters, these daughters of the Lidingo family. And while they would never forget their own parents, she knew how fortunate they were to have *Rav* and *Rebbetzin* Jacobson and Mr. and Mrs. Igell as parents now. Loving and devoted, they understood the unique situation of the girls in their care so well! Despite the difficulties, they had the wisdom and boundless patience to say the right thing in the right way, at the right time. Brachie was right - this was the greatest treasure she could ask for right now.

Hella

Hella arrived in Lidingo alone. She was tall and thin, with sharp, high cheekbones. Her eyes revealed nothing: looking into them was like looking into an abyss. Her closely cropped hair added to the severity of her appearance.

From the very first day, it was clear that she was different. She guarded her spot in the dining room obsessively, and never joined the other girls when they played or laughed. Instead, she spent her free time silently reciting Psalms, throwing her whole heart into the prayers whose words were a balm for her soul.

At times, some of the girls, who had put their fears behind them and become close friends, sensed Hella's distress and attempted to bring her into their circle. They invited her to their rooms, and tried to persuade her to join them in lighthearted activities which they hoped would bring a smile to her sad face. But it was as if an iron wall separated them from Hella: she acknowledged the invitations with a small smile, and refused them with a shrug of her shoulders.

Hella was punctual to a fault, be it to classes, meals, or prayers. Her notebooks were a model of perfect order. She sat quietly and obediently through class, listening, but never actively participating. On rare occasions, a tiny spark in her eyes hinted at understanding, agreement, or perhaps a flash of memory from another world; no one knew exactly which. The staff at Lidingo was very considerate. They waited patiently for time, the great healer, to work its magic, and did not make any demands on Hella. The girls, powerless to help her, could only honor Hella's wishes and leave her alone.

Hella shared a room with Marinka, Rocheleh, Rivka, and Malka, a lovely group of experienced, understanding older girls. Mrs. Igell hoped that the day would come when she would open up to at least one of them, but their overtures were firmly if politely rebuffed.

Quite naturally in a dormitory full of girls, there was a long line for the shower every night. No one really minded the wait, though, since the time on line was pleasantly spent. From the early hours of the evening, the halls rang with jokes and laughter, punctuated by cries of "I'm next!" or "I'm after her!" They milled around with their towels and soap, talking or singing while they waited. Sometimes they sang the songs they all knew and loved; at other times, someone offered to teach a new one. Many of Lidingo's special songs were composed and numerous plans for parties and special events were hatched during these hours of camaraderie.

At first, no one noticed that Hella did not join the line for the shower. When her roommates did, they assumed that, reserved, as they knew her to be, she preferred to shower later on, when everyone had gone to sleep. Malka had even heard her walking around at night while she had feigned sleep. The matter passed without comment, as did many of Hella's actions. Most of the girls found Hella's presence and mannerisms troubling, and chose to ignore both. They hoped that with time, she would finally adjust.

Rivka was the first to notice the unpleasant smell coming from Hella's direction, but beyond an occasional furtive glance, she did nothing. She was not going to be the one to raise the subject, certainly not in public! Marinka and Rocheleh also became aware of the strange smell, and decided, each on her own, to keep quiet. Malka, whose sense of smell was very poor, was the only one who noticed nothing unusual.

In the month of Elul, with Rosh Hashanah fast approaching, special emphasis was placed in class on the commandments between man and his fellow, among them the prohibitions against *lashon hara, rechilus,* and embarrassing others. Each girl tried to work on herself, and did her best to avoid these transgressions. Hella's roommates had plenty of opportunity to perfect themselves in all three areas. Rather than embarrass Hella, they would pull their blankets up over their heads at night and bear with the smell. Rivka took the added precaution of keeping a bar of soap on her pillow to mask the odor in the room.

One day, the girls were informed that morning classes had been cancelled, and they were free to do as they pleased until the Rebbetzin's class in the afternoon. Rivka, Malka, Marinka, and Rocheleh went up to their room while Hella, as usual, stayed behind in the classroom, fervently reciting Psalms. At first, they busied themselves with their own affairs, pausing only for an occasional thoughtful glance at Hella's bed. No one spoke.

Rivka finished what she was doing and sat down rather abruptly on her bed. Malka looked at her questioningly, but there was no response from Rivka. The high spirited chatter from the nearby rooms and the lively commotion of games being played on the ground floor were a stark contrast to the uneasy quiet in the room. Malka broke the silence.

"What's wrong?" she asked, looking at Rivka.

"Nothing," answered Rivka.

"Then why are you so quiet?" Malka persisted.

"I'm thinking."

"Something good?"

"It could be," said Rivka.

Marinka and Rocheleh came to sit next to Rivka. "What 'could be' good?" they asked.

Rivka chose her words carefully. "We all can see that Hella is lonely and unhappy, but she won't let us near her. So I had an idea... maybe it would help."

Hella's roommates had come to view her as their group's personal problem. If there was something that would cheer her up, they wanted to hear about it. "What's your idea?" they asked.

"Well," said Rivka hesitantly, "I just thought... maybe... tell me what you think... maybe we could buy Hella a present for Rosh Hashanah? Do you think she would like that? Do you think it would make her happy?"

"A present? But we don't have any money!" Rocheleh blurted out.

"Yes we do! We all get a weekly allowance. Why can't we put aside something for a gift for Hella?" Rivka said.

"But it's so little," protested Malka.

Rivka refused to give up. "All right," she said, "So we'll buy something small, just a token."

"What do you think we could afford?" asked Marinka, warming to the idea.

"Let's think," said Rocheleh, "Any suggestions?"

"I have an idea," said Rivka, hesitant again.

"Let's hear it," they all said, convinced by now that any idea of Rivka's must be a good one.

"No. I'm not going to tell you. Instead, let's do this: each of us will write her suggestion on a piece of paper. We won't put our names on the papers. Then we'll look at them and decide, without knowing who wrote what. Do you agree?"

They did. With furrowed brows, they considered different possibilities, and then made their decisions. They handed their small, folded slips of paper to Rivka, who tossed them in the palm of her hand. Each girl picked one up to read aloud.

Rocheleh was first. "Let's see," she said, "It says soap," she announced.

Next was Marinka. "This one says -" she looked at the crumpled paper in her hand - "Soap."

Rivka read the third choice. "A pen," she said.

Malka unfolded the last piece of paper. "Soap," she whispered.

The girls looked at each other. The room was uncomfortably quiet as each one realized that the others shared her feelings. The only one who was really surprised was Malka.

"I don't get it," she said bluntly, "Why soap? There's plenty of soap here. Why should we buy that as a gift for Hella?"

Marinka was the first to recover. "Listen, Malka," she began gently, "We know that everything G-d does, He does for good. But sometimes we have the opportunity to actually see it for ourselves. Like now, for example."

"Oh, Marinka, I know all that. But what does that have to do with soap?"

Marinka did not give up. She took a pleasantly scented bar of soap off her shelf and handed it to Malka. "Take a sniff. Can you smell it?"

Malka shook her head; she couldn't smell a thing.

"Don't you see? You don't smell anything: not good smells, and not bad ones... That's why you didn't notice."

They all started talking at once, trying to explain to Malka why they had all chosen soap. Eventually, despite all the confusion and noise, Malka finally understood what the problem was. They all decided that they would buy some soap for Hella, and leave it on her pillow with a nice note. They hoped their surprise would bring a touch of happiness to their sad roommate's closed heart.

The Gift

It was the day before Rosh Hashanah, the day of judgment when every individual's actions, the good and the bad, are weighed before the heavenly Throne. Would it be a year of life or death, health or sickness, success or failure? All would be judged on Rosh Hashanah. For the girls of Lidingo, these were truly days of awe. They, who had suffered through the torments of the Holocaust, now had to grapple with the age-old question of why the righteous suffer while the wicked prosper. Their memories were fresh and vivid: the shocked refusal to believe that anything bad could really happen, followed by the horrors which proved to be all too real. They could not forget their loved ones, inscribed for death together with millions of their brethren, while others, inscribed for life, were miraculously saved. Can any mortal man fathom the Al-mighty's wisdom, merciful even as it chastises the righteous? If there was anyone who understood the true significance of G-d's judgement on Rosh Hashanah, it was these girls, who had seen Jews led to the gas chambers and the crematoria.

The Rebbetzin did her best to lift their spirits by emphasizing that Rosh Hashanah is not only the Day of Judgment but also a holiday. Yet the girls' mood was serious and contemplative. Their minds were on man's insignificance compared to G-d's greatness. They poured out their hearts before Him, begging Him to show mercy on His people from now to eternity.

Hella was completely caught up in the atmosphere of *erev Rosh Hashanah*, and was more withdrawn than ever. After morning prayers, the Rebbetzin announced that there would be no classes that day, to allow them time to prepare for the holiday. Hella returned to her room, where she found a small box on her bed.

"What's this?" she wondered aloud, "Who could have left it here?"

Then she saw the note: "To our dear Hella, with love from your roommates."

That's interesting, she thought. The girls were waiting out in the hall, eager to hear her reaction and share in her pleasure. Hella opened the box, and the world went black. Soap! Merciful Father, anything but soap... To her friends' amazement, she burst into high pitched, hysterical screams. "Soap!" she cried, "Murderers!"

The small object which held so much terror for Hella clattered to the floor. "Oh my G-d, why have You done this to me? Soap!" Hella broke down altogether, and cried uncontrollably.

Her roommates recovered from their initial shock and hurried in to the room. Hella was sitting on her bed, her face buried in her hands.

"Hella darling, we're so sorry," they whispered, "We didn't mean to hurt you. We didn't know you were afraid of soap," they stammered helplessly.

Hella stopped sobbing and raised her head. A silent accusation stared out of her tear filled eyes: You? How could you do this to me? In a strangled voice the girls had never heard, she burst out, "This is soap! A Jew is forbidden to wash with soap!

The "showers" in the gas chambers

It's saturated with Jewish blood, with the flesh of old people and children. Do you know how they made soap? They made it from the holy bodies of my father and mother, my brothers and sisters, my uncles and aunts, and everyone, everyone. It is forbidden! Forbidden! Forbidden!" And she cried...

Hella's roommates hovered over her, petrified. Several other girls, who had heard the screams and rushed in to help, backed out into the hall, shocked and frightened. They were deathly quiet, almost afraid to breathe.

Suddenly Hella spoke. "We were in the bunker for five days," she said in a dull, flat voice, oblivious to those around her. It was the first time anyone had heard her speak about herself. "My baby brother, our Yitzchakele, was only ten months old, and he had a terrible cough. An Aktion had taken place in the ghetto. After everyone had gone, we heard German soldiers talking, right above our heads. At that very moment, Yitzchakele started coughing. It didn't take long after that; they found our bunker easily. Father, Mother, Chaim, Suri, Yitzchakele and I were chased with clubs from the bunker to the Umschlagplatz, a big square in town where they rounded up people for deportation. All the others who had been caught were already there, waiting for the transport. Chaim, Suri and Yitzchakele were taken from us immediately and shot before our eyes - they were of no use to the Germans. Mother held me close and said, `Hella, you will survive and tell everyone what happened to us.'

"They sent us to a labor camp. That was the last I saw of Father. At first I was with Mother, until they grabbed me away from her and sent me to the girls' barracks. They killed Mother, along with all the others, and I had no one left. Then they pulled the gold teeth out of their mouths, and made soap from their holy bodies.

"Anyone who couldn't work anymore was sent to the gas chambers. They sent me there too. We were forced inside a shower room and given pieces of soap. Then we were ordered to turn on the shower heads..."

The girls shuddered.

"But G-d in His wisdom wanted me to live, and a miracle happened. Something went wrong with the mechanism, and we were saved." Her voice rose in an unnatural shriek as she cried, "I can never take a shower, never! No soap! No shower!"

No one had noticed Rebbetzin Jacobson among the crowd listening to Hella's story. "Hella," she said gently, "I want you to come downstairs with me. There are some things we have to talk about."

The Rebbetzin's quiet confidence and inner tranquility had their usual compelling effect. Hella regained her composure. With a grateful look, she followed the Rebbetzin out of the room.

No one ever knew just what the Rebbetzin told her, but one thing was obvious: something in Hella changed. She was much calmer, and began to open up to the people around her. She also became one of the Rebbetzin's most ardent admirers.

Rivka, always the practical one, hung a poster in the hall inscribed with a saying from our Sages: "Do not judge your fellow until you stand in his place." It was a lesson the girls engraved upon their hearts.

Missing Relatives

It was only natural that the girls could not simply put the past behind them and forgot about what they had experienced during the war. Instead, with help of the Lidingo family, they attempted to open a new chapter in their lives, built upon the ruins of the past. The first step was the painful search for surviving relatives. Each of them knew that certain relatives were definitely gone, whether because they had seen them killed or because they had heard the news from others who had watched them die. However, there were many instances in which the fate of family members was unknown. The hope still lingered that perhaps they were still alive.

Newly established information centers compiled listings of names and addresses of survivors to aid the refugees in their search for their families. Everyone registered at these centers in the hope that at least part of the family would be reunited. Hope was always there; at times it was replaced by bitter disappointment. In addition, Rav Jacobson, Rav Shlomo Wolbe and R. Israel Chasdan visited the camps to search for any surviving relatives of the Lidingo girls. Their efforts meant the world to the lonely girls.

Esther was a girl who knew how to put up a good front. By day, she smiled and laughed, but at night, her pillow was wet with tears. She had been searching for relatives for three months, with absolutely no results. She simply could not believe that every last member of her family had been killed, and that she was the only survivor. With each passing day, despair ate deeper and deeper into her heart. One afternoon, she returned from one of her frequent visits to the information center in obvious distress. On the way to her room, she ran into Rebbetzin Jacobson. She was terribly upset but did not want the Rebbetzin, who was always so concerned for them all, to know. She tried to avoid the Rebbetzin's gaze, but it was impossible to escape her knowing, watchful eyes.

"What's wrong, Esther?" asked the Rebbetzin, "Why do you look so unhappy?"

Esther made a supreme effort to put a smile on her face. It didn't work. As it was, her tears were barely contained. Now they streamed from her eyes unchecked, as months of suffering, so carefully concealed until that moment, flowed from her heart down her cheeks.

Without saying a word, the Rebbetzin stroked Esther's hair and took her to her room. She gave her a drink and waited for the tears to spend themselves naturally. She knew that at times like this, crying would help alleviate the pain.

Esther pulled herself together. She wiped her eyes and tried to apologize for her outburst. She was uncomfortable about making a scene in front of the Rebbetzin; where was her self-control? But one look at the Rebbetzin's eyes told her that there was no need to apologize.

When the Rebbetzin saw that Esther had calmed down, she asked again what was troubling her.

"I didn't find anyone." The Rebbetzin knew enough to understand what she was talking about. "I don't have a single soul in the whole world. My entire family was killed by the Nazis," she said, making an effort to keep her voice steady.

The Rebbetzin put a hand on Esther's shoulder. "Esther, there are many people who survived the war and are still alive but haven't registered with the centers, whether because they don't know about them, or because they're afraid of having their names on any sort of list. Don't give in to despair. Trust in G-d. You may yet find family some day. You have to remember that G-'s ways are lovingkindness and truth, and that everything that happens is for the best."

"Yes," interrupted Esther, "But - why? Why, of all my family, did I have to be the only one to stay alive? I would gladly have given my life to save my mother, my father, my brothers and sisters. Why was I the one to be saved? What for?"

"Esther, Esther, that's your grief stricken heart talking, not your head. First of all, we still are not one hundred percent sure of what happened, you know. But whatever the outcome of your search is, there's one thing we all have to understand and accept. We do not know G-d's reasons. Only He is the One who gives life, and He is the One who takes it from us. As for why you alone were kept alive, I'm sure you can answer that yourself: to continue your family's heritage, to live the way you were raised, to pray for your family's souls, and to live proudly as a *Torah* Jewess."

"Alone?" Esther blurted out.

"Alone?" repeated the Rebbetzin, "Are you really alone, Esther? We're your family now, a big family with parents who love you, and many, many daughters. All the girls here in Lidingo are your sisters who care about you. What other family do you know that has over one hundred members?"

The Rebbetzin succeeded in putting a smile on Esther's face. She could not have been more correct: all the girls in Lidingo were Esther's sisters. How lucky she was to be part of such a wonderful family... as much as she longed for her loved ones, she thanked G-d for giving her this new home.

A few months later, a young woman arrived in Lidingo. She was a relative of Esther's. Her health was very poor, and she was clearly in need of medical care. She spent several months in Lidingo recuperating. With the girls' blessings, the two of them eventually left Lidingo together, promising to stay in touch with their sisters.

* * *

Sara and Marinka had lost their parents in the Lodz ghetto. The Germans were looking for girls and women with small fingers who could handle the small, delicate components of precision instruments. When they asked Sara and Marinka if they had experience in that type of work, they said yes, and were sent to the Siemens plant. The sisters lived in constant fear that each day in the plant was their last, and they were right. One day, they were transferred to Ravensbruck.

A group of girls on their way to a lesson

At thirteen, Marinka was an exceptionally beautiful girl. A female SS officer stared at her constantly, unable to accept the fact that a Jewish girl could be so pretty. One day she approached her and said, "Marinka, you are not a Jewess!"

Marinka did not lose her cool. "I am a Jewess!" she replied.

"No, that's impossible.

You must be a mischling," the SS woman insisted stubbornly.

"I am not a mischling, I am a Jewess," repeated Marinka. Marinka was fully aware that her truthful answer was not in her best interests. At a time when Jews looked death in the eye a thousand times a day, when hunger caused people to literally lose their minds, Marinka could easily have answered differently and saved herself much suffering. But Marinka would not have dreamed of denying her people; under the most difficult circumstances imaginable, this young teenager withstood enormous temptation.

Together, Marinka and Sara survived the war. They knew their parents were gone, but they heard that their uncle had also survived. They wrote to the mayor of Lodz, telling him they were alive and asking that any relatives who inquired about them be given their address in Sweden. After their uncle was liberated from Transnistria, he too contacted the mayor, who passed on the message. He sent them a two word telegram: Letter follows.

Not long afterwards, Sara and Marinka received a long letter from their uncle, in which he told them about Rav Jacobson and insisted that they go to see him. In the meantime, they heard about Lidingo from other sources as well. When they visited the school on Pesach, they decided to stay.

Rav Wolbe was later to say that anyone who wanted to see a shining example of happiness with one's lot should go to Marinka. Today, the two sisters are active, happy wives and mothers with wonderful families of their own.

Chanke

The purchase of new clothing was a special occasion in Lidingo. Mrs. Igell, whose wise and watchful eyes looked after the girls' needs, was also responsible for their clothing. If she noticed that someone had outgrown her coat, for example, she immediately took the matter in hand. She would invite the girl to join her on a trip into Stockholm, where they would go shopping for a new coat, which the excited girl would personally select and try on. It would, Mrs. Igell pointed out, be a brand new coat which would be hers alone. For these girls, who had come to Lidingo in old, shabby, ill-fitting hand-me-downs, this was a beautiful dream come true. Mrs. Igell would not allow any hint of the school's heavy monetary burden to mar these lovely outings. Blissfully unaware of the financial difficulties entailed, the girls basked in the feeling that someone cared enough to pamper them.

When Chanke arrived in Lidingo, she was a small, thin girl wearing a pathetically oversized dress and shoes. She was greeted by Mrs. Igell, who took the frightened girl's hand in hers and held her close.

"Chanke," she told her, "From now on, you are a member of a big, loving family, our Lidingo family. All of us are happy that you have come here and hope that you will enjoy being with us."

They entered the dining room together. The clatter of the plates and the chatter of the girls stopped at once as everyone turned to look at the new arrival.

"Girls," said Mrs. Igell, "Meet a new member of the family, Chanke. We have a new sister. *Mazal tov!*"

Cries of "*Mazal tov!* Welcome!" were heard from all sides. The girls waved hello to Chanke and smiled at her. When the meal was over, they came over to say hello. One look was all it took. They too had suffered the embarrassment of clothing that was too big or too small - any size but their own. A group of girls who were about Chanke's size quickly got together to lend her proper clothes.

But to everyone's surprise, Chanke clung to her clothes, refusing to part with her outsize rags. Not long afterwards, parcels of clothing donated by various charitable organizations arrived in Lidingo. There were a number of nice dresses in Chanke's size, but she refused to even look at them; all of Mrs. Igell's efforts to persuade her to take something were fruitless.

The simplest thing would have been to take Chanke on a shopping trip in town, but Lidingo's budget did not allow it at that time. The school had received some funding, but it was woefully insufficient to cover Lidingo's entire budget, and Rav Jacobson was forced to make repeated fund raising trips abroad. However, the costs of providing for all the needs of girls, who had come to Lidingo with only the rags on their backs, were enormous, and the institution suffered from a perpetual deficit.* The girls were kept blissfully innocent of the school's financial problems, as the staff wished to preserve their hard-won good spirits, regardless of the cost. This did mean, though, that Mrs. Igell could not immediately take Chanke out shopping.

---

* Initially, Lidingo was fully supported by the Swedish government. Starting from October, 1946, the government provided funding only for girls under the age of sixteen. Since most of the girls were over sixteen, this effectively eliminated most of Lidingo's budget. Rabbi Charles Ullmann of the Rescue Children's Fund in America came to the aid of the institution and funded it for the following two years. After that, the American Joint Distribution Committee assumed the burden of providing for the girls until they went to Eretz Yisrael.

Eventually a sum of money came in, and it was allocated for Chanke. Mrs. Igell cheerfully informed her that they were going shopping the next day, just the two of them.

The girls who had been in Lidingo long enough to understand what this meant cast envious looks at Chanke; they knew that she was in for a real treat. Going shopping with Mrs. Igell was nothing less than a celebration! Not only would she have Mrs. Igell's undivided attention for the day,

she would also have the fun of a trip to the city to window shop and decide what she wanted to buy. But Chanke did not share in their excitement. Deep distrust and suspicion still would not allow her to lower her guard and be happy. But she did like Mrs. Igell, so she agreed to go along, and hoped that the trip would be a pleasant one.

On the way to the city, Mrs. Igell tried to get Chanke to talk about what kind of clothes she would like to buy, hoping to coax a response out of the quiet girl. But Chanke just looked at her wordlessly. When they reached the store, Mrs. Igell tried again.

"Look, Chanke, these are just your size," she said, pointing to a rack of attractive new dresses, "Choose one that you like. We'll buy whatever you want."

Chanke obediently stepped over to the rack of dresses. She examined them over and over. Finally, she pointed hesitantly to a pretty blue dress with red stripes and a white collar.

"I like this one too," said Mrs. Igell, pleased to see Chanke finally showing some interest, "Go ahead and try it on!"

Chanke did not move.

"What's wrong, Chanke? There's a fitting room right here. I'll wait for you while you try on the dress," Mrs. Igell encouraged her.

"No!" hissed Chanke, "I'm not taking this dress off," she insisted, clutching at her old one.

"Chanke," said Mrs. Igell patiently, "That dress is far too big for you and it's all worn out. We've come all the way to town just to buy you a new dress. Look what a pretty outfit you've chosen! Let's throw away the old one - I can't wait to see how the new one looks on you." Her tone was gentle and persuasive, but it was no use.

"No!" replied Chanke emphatically. But, tempted by the beautiful new outfit, her resolve began to waver. She looked around her and then said quietly to Mrs. Igell, "Come here. I'll whisper, so they won't hear."

"Yes?" By now, there was very little that could surprise Mrs. Igell.

"They'll take my dress away," Chanke whispered furtively.

"Who are `they'?" asked Mrs. Igell.

"They!" cried Chanke in a chilling voice. "I had a dress and a nice sweater and they took them away from me, and gave me a big man's shirt, and I was cold... Then the kapo felt sorry for me and gave me this dress. She told me to take good care of it and not give it to anyone. If I take it off, they'll take it away from me, and I'll have nothing to wear again."

Mrs. Igell hugged the frightened little girl. "My darling Chanke, don't be afraid. No one will take your dress away. I'll watch it for you while you try on the new one, and we'll also buy you a new skirt and blouse and shoes. Everything will be yours, in your size, and no one will take them from you."

"And you won't throw my dress away?" Chanke asked.

"The day that you ask me to throw it out, I will do so. Until then, I will guard it for you faithfully, *bli neder*."

Chanke was still unsure. After thinking the matter over, she decided that she could trust Mrs. Igell, and the dress was tried on and purchased. The same doubts, questions, promises, and assurances were repeated all over with each new item of clothing Mrs. Igell urged Chanke to buy that day. Her confidence grew with each new acquisition. By the time they picked out a new pair of shoes, Chanke was completely relaxed.

Twinkling stars accompanied a happy pair back to Lidingo: a smartly dressed young girl and an exhausted woman, both highly satisfied with the outcome of the day's efforts. For the first time in years, Chanke hummed a tune as she walked alongside Mrs. Igell. And why not? She had been reborn.

A Cry in the Night

The silence of a snowy January night was shattered by a cry from one of the rooms. Mrs. Igell awoke at once. "What was that?" she said aloud.

But the dormitory was silent. Mrs. Igell decided that she must have been dreaming, and tried to go back to sleep. Just as her eyes began to close, she heard it again. Wide awake now, she knew it had not been a dream; she would have to investigate. She threw on her robe and hurried up the stairs, where she met the Rebbetzin, who had also been awakened by the noise.

And then they heard it again.

Who could it be? Nighttime disturbances had been a common problem until their doctor had prescribed tranquilizers for any girls who had difficulty sleeping. Since then, they had all slept peacefully - until tonight. Exchanging silent looks, the two women went upstairs. The rustling of their robes and the padding of their slippers seemed very loud in the quiet building. Upstairs, they found ten frightened girls sitting up in their beds, still half-asleep.

"Who screamed?" asked the Rebbetzin.

"Rivka," said Malka.

Rivka? She, of all the girls? Strong willed, high spirited Rivka was the last one they would have thought of. From the day she had come to Lidingo, there had never been any problems with Rivka. She had adjusted easily and well to the new environment, and was an excellent student. In fact, she was a good example for many of the other girls. She radiated tranquility and peace of mind, and had been given many important tasks in the school's social life. She had accepted them good-naturedly, as she was happy to help out. Mrs. Igell and the Rebbetzin could see that while the girls were surprised by her sudden outburst, they were simply too tired to react.

"Please go back to bed, girls," said the Rebbetzin, "Rivka would feel very bad if she knew that so many girls were involved. Malka, Marinka, Hella, and Rocheleh," she said to Rivka's roommates, "I want you to find another place to sleep tonight, so some of the girls in the other rooms will have to double up. Who's willing to help out?" she asked, looking around.

There was no shortage of volunteers, and the girls quickly vanished into nearby rooms. The Rebbetzin and Mrs. Igell went to check on Rivka. They found her sitting on her bed. She turned to them as soon as they came in.

"So that's it. You're here," she said in a strange voice. "I knew that you would come to get me in the end." There was an odd, glazed look in her eyes, as if the two women in front of her were ghosts.

"Did you really think I wouldn't recognize you? Every night you threaten me, and now you've finally come. Why are you just standing there?" she asked hoarsely. "Go ahead. Shoot me and I'll die, once and for all. Just give me a few minutes to say *Viduy* and *Shma Yisrael.* Then you can tell everyone that Nazis know Jewish prayers." Her face twisted as her voice rose higher and higher.

"If you really must know, it's all because of Sosha. She couldn't stand the pain and she screamed. Don't look so surprised," she said bitterly, "You should know. You're the ones who gave her thirty lashes when they caught her with a piece of dry bread in her pocket!"

Suddenly she jumped up and walked over to the Rebbetzin. "Curse you, you monster! You should all be burned alive! Why don't you kill me now, right here? Don't look at me like that. You know you killed them all, poor Papa, and Mama, who was so sick - all of them! I - I don't care what happens anymore!"

The Rebbetzin and Mrs. Igell didn't say a word. They knew that this monologue, coming from the depths of Rivka's heart and mind, was the best therapy for the girl, who had kept her pain and fears bottled up until now. It would be better to get it all out of her system.

"Shema Yisrael, Hashem Elokeinu, Hashem Echod!" she cried out, and fell back on her bed, unconscious.

The Rebbetzin hovered over her while Mrs. Igell ran to get a glass of water. A few minutes later, Rivka regained consciousness. A gentle hand on her forehead showed that she was burning with fever. They watched helplessly as she shook with violent chills, and her teeth began to chatter. She mumbled incessantly, but it was impossible to understand what she was saying. They eased a thermometer into her mouth; it registered 40.5 degrees (104.9 Fahrenheit). They helped her swallow some aspirin and covered her.

"Rebbetzin, go back to your room," said Mrs. Igell quietly, "You can't sit here all night. You have to teach tomorrow."

The Rebbetzin grudgingly agreed. "But promise me you'll wake me immediately if anything happens," she insisted. Mrs. Igell assured her that she would.

Shortly afterwards, Rivka stopped shaking and appeared to be more comfortable. Her breathing became rhythmic as she dozed off into a restful sleep. Mrs. Igell was relieved to see that she looked better, but she still remained at her side until morning.

The next day, no one talked about what had happened to Rivka. The girls tried hard not to embarrass others and avoid *lashon hara*, and they knew it would make her very unhappy to be the topic of idle gossip. They all liked Rivka, and were happy to hear that she was feeling better. A few days later, Rivka recovered completely and returned to her normal routine. Those who knew about what had happened kept silent, and it almost seemed as if the entire incident had never taken place.

About half a year later, when Rivka'a illness was history, Rivka awoke up one morning confused and disoriented. After washing her hands, she turned to her roommate, Malka. "It's the strangest thing, Malka, but I just had the most dreadful dream."

"What did you dream?" asked Malka sympathetically.

"I'm not even sure... it was a real nightmare, all mixed up. I was with my friend from the camps, Sosha. She had some old bread in her pocket, and she got a terrible beating from the kapo. She was covered with bruises, and had these terrible bloody red lines all over her body." She shuddered at the memory.

"It sounds awful," said Malka. Nightmares were something they could all relate to. "What happened after that?"

"The next part was really strange: Sosha screamed, and two SS guards came in. I don't know what exactly I was doing, but they caught me too. I looked at them, and they looked just like the Rebbetzin and Mrs. Igell. It was horrible. How could anyone have such a dream?" she said, burying her face in her hands. Her voice was muffled as she continued her story. "I told them everything, and I was sure they would kill me, but they didn't do anything. They didn't even talk. I just don't understand it..." her voice trailed off.

"That really was strange," agreed Malka - and Rivka was never the wiser.

Lidingo's Little Girl

One day a young man appeared at Lidingo's front door, holding the hand of a little four year old girl in one of his, and a big suitcase in the other. He was visibly hesitant as he approached the building, and looked around with a mixture of curiosity and apprehension. The little girl who gripped his hand so tightly was obviously fearful, and clearly unhappy about being there. The grounds were deserted, as everyone was in the dining room enjoying the delicious lunch prepared by Mrs. Winkler and her cooking staff. The young man had no way of knowing that, however; mealtimes in Lidingo were quiet and relaxed, and no telltale noises escaped the building.

"There's no point in just standing around here," he told himself, "Knock and get it over with." He had been told to speak to "the Rebbetzin," and if there actually was someone inside the quiet house, that was whom he would ask for. While he waited to see if anyone was home, he took a good look at the building, noting that it urgently needed a coat of paint, and that several of the windows were in various states of disrepair. At the same time, however, he was impressed by the aura of cleanliness and order that emanated from the simple structure.

As it happened, the Rebbetzin herself came to the door. "How may I help you, sir?" she said politely.

The young man was startled. "Uh... I'm looking for the, uh, the Rebbetzin," he stammered.

"Certainly," she said, "Please come in." She smiled as she looked at the little girl, but wondered why he had come. There were people who had come to Lidingo in search of relatives, but this did not appear to be the case now. "What can I do for you?" she asked when they were seated inside.

"Well," he began uncomfortably, "My name is Avraham Levi, and this," he said, pointing to the little girl, "Is my niece, Lenka. Her mother was... is... my sister. I'm originally from Lodz."

Lenka stood behind him, looking as if she wanted to disappear. The Rebbetzin understood from the accusing expression on her tiny face that she was extremely frightened.

Mr. Levi tapped his fingers nervously. "I won't waste the Rebbetzin's time with stories about what happened to me during the war. I'll only say this: with G-d's help, I was saved from certain death more than once." He stared blankly at the wall and continued, talking more to himself than to her. "The news of the liberation reached us when we were already standing on line for the gas chambers. Since then, I've been searching for my family, but except for Lenka here, I haven't found even one single person left alive. My parents both died early on. My father was beaten to death," he said with obvious pain, "And I found out afterwards that my mother died of disease and fatigue. There was no trace of my only sister -I have no idea if she's still alive. The search for her gave me no rest. From the moment I woke up in the morning until I fell asleep at night, I couldn't stop thinking about her.

"One night, after an exhausting and utterly fruitless day, I fell into bed, crushed and dejected. I fell asleep immediately, and then - the miracle happened. I had a dream, in which my sister Sara came to me with a baby girl in her arms. It was Lenka, a beautiful little one-year-old, the family favorite. Sara looked very sad as she stood there, holding her. Suddenly the baby fell from her arms and started crying. Instead of picking her up, Sara screamed, `Avrum, Avrum, save my baby!' To this day, I can still hear those screams. I woke up in a cold sweat. It was one o'clock in the morning, but I couldn't get back to sleep. The dream played itself out before my eyes again and again, and I could see Lenka as clearly as if she had been in the room with me. Then, all at once, I remembered everything.

"Sara had heard there was going to be a selection in the ghetto. She smuggled Lenka out to the Aryan side and brought her to a Christian family named Stanislav, good customers of our family's grocery store before the war. We all knew them. They were childless and took Lenka gladly. Sara gave them all her gold jewelry and whatever money she had. The only thing she asked them to keep for Lenka was a gold chain and a tiny charm engraved with the word `*Yerushalayim*.' She begged them to look after Lenka until she returned, and forced herself to run off without a backward glance. I met her on the way to the Umschlagplatz and she told me what she had done. She cried as if she would never stop, and made me promise that if I survived, I wouldn't forget her precious Lenka. I promised her that if I was still alive, I would come back for Lenka and take care of her, no matter what."

Mr. Levi fell silent, his throat constricted with emotion. The Rebbetzin wordlessly handed him a glass of water. He recited the blessing, took a few sips, and continued his story.

"From that moment, I knew no rest. I waited impatiently for daybreak, so that I could go to the Stanislavs. I was sure that it was just a matter of hours before I would scoop our Lenka up in my arms and take her away with me.

"I had no problem finding their house, even though it looked very different than it had before the war. It used to be an attractive, well-kept cottage, with a flourishing green garden in front. Now the garden was neglected and infested with weeds, and the house itself was shabby, with stained, peeling paint. It seems the war took its toll on the house as well. But who cared about the house, I told myself. What mattered was Lenka.

"As I knocked on the door, I suddenly wasn't so sure of myself anymore. Mrs. Stanislav blocked the entrance, but I could see that behind her, sitting on the floor playing with a doll, was a little girl, about four years old. Despite the shabby surroundings, the girl looked very well cared for. Her cheeks were rosy and she was wearing nice clothes. My heart almost burst with excitement at the sight of her, but the child barely looked at me.

"`Mother, who is that?' she asked, pointing at me.

"`Shh, *Mamushka*, it isn't polite to point like that, is it?' said Mrs. Stanislav.

"I can't say that I recognized her. She had been a baby when I saw her last, and three years is a long time at that age. But I knew for sure that it was Lenka. I was at a loss for words. It was obvious how close the two of them were, and suddenly, I was afraid. All too soon, I learned that my fears were well-founded.

"I introduced myself to Mrs. Stanislav and she invited me in. We sat at the table and I told her my story. She did not deny anything. `Look what good care I've taken of her,' she said proudly, `*Mamushka* is my own darling daughter now.' She was perfectly calm and quite pleased with herself. I was horrified. This woman was referring to my niece as her daughter!

"'Yes,' I told her carefully, 'That's obvious. I see how good she looks, and I'm very grateful. I can't thank you enough for what you've done for our family. I hope that the money my sister left with you was enough for all of Lenka's needs.'

"`Oh, yes,' Mrs. Stanislav interrupted me, `It was more than enough. Just look at the cupboard, at the sink, at the curtains, at the food in the pantry. It's all thanks to your poor late sister,' she said piously, and crossed herself.

"She was talking as if my sister was already dead, while I was still doing everything in my power to find her alive! I saw that I had no choice. This woman either did not understand, or else did not want to understand, why I had come. I would have to spell it out clearly. `Thank G-d, the war is over now,' I said to her, `And I've come to get my niece, as I promised my sister the day she brought her to you.'

"Mrs. Stanislav froze and her friendliness evaporated. Apparently, when she let me in she hadn't a clue as to the purpose of my visit. She must have thought that I came to see the new sink and the curtains. She started screaming.

"`Never!'" she shouted, `I'll never give her up, never! Do you hear? Do you think I raised her all these years for nothing?' She pointed a shaking finger at the shocked child. `I fed her and clothed her and now you want to just take her away? Forget it! Get out!'

"`For nothing,' I thought bitterly. She just finished boasting about living on my sister's money, and all of a sudden it was for nothing. But she wasn't done yet.

"`That's the way it is with you dirty Jews,' she hissed, `I knew it all along. I always taught my *Mamushka* to watch out for Jews, and now you've come to steal her!'

"This was the first time *Mamushka* really took a good look at me. She gave me an angry glare of utter hostility; many more were to follow.

"My initial joy at seeing my niece was gone. Perhaps I was naive, but I never dreamed that I would encounter such blunt, total refusal. I waited for the woman to calm down, and then I said something which I hoped would soften her resistance. 'I am willing to pay any amount you ask if you'll give me the child. You will be able to buy many beautiful things for yourself and for the house if you allow me to take her back to live among Jews.'

"'Jews - pfooy.' The woman spat and crossed herself. 'My *Mamushka* is a good Christian. Show the uncle your cross,' she said. *Mamushka* obeyed instantly. She showed me a crucifix and kissed it.

"My heart sank. What could I do? I tried again. 'You know what? When your husband returns, tell him about our meeting and my offer. Remember: whatever you want - in exchange for the girl,' I said in the most convincing voice I could muster.

"'Forget it. It's out of the question,' she said harshly, 'Please leave now.'

"When I hesitated, she almost threw me out of the house. I had no choice but to leave, without Lenka. I started walking, too miserable to care where my feet were taking me. I spent hours wandering through Lodz, trying to come to grips with the awful reality. At long last I had found someone from the family, my beloved niece, and she might as well have been on another planet. But I was determined not to give up. Whatever it took, I would get Lenka away from the Stanislavs.

"I timed my next visit for the evening, when Mr. Stanislav would be home. At first, he also wouldn't hear of my offer, but then he said something which shocked me.

"'Everyone knows you Jews are all sorcerers,' he began.

It was hard not to laugh. If we were all sorcerers, how had the Nazis managed to kill so many of us? But I didn't say anything, hoping that this might be an opening for me to get Lenka.

"'I'll make a deal with you. Use some of your Jew sorcery and make my wife give birth to a boy - a boy, mind you, not a girl. If you can do that, I will give you the girl for 30,000 zlotys. Otherwise, there is nothing to talk about.'

"Believe me," Avraham told the Rebbetzin, "From that moment on, I prayed three times a day that Mrs. Stanislav, who had been married for years and had no children, would have a boy. I stayed in Lodz, and from time to time I would visit them, hoping... Two weeks ago, I went past their house, and I decided to go in. This time Mr. Stanislav was glad to see me.

"'It's just like I said!' he greeted me, beaming, `The Jews are sorcerers! My wife is going to have a baby!' he announced happily.

"I made no effort to hide my excitement. `So I can take my niece with me now,' I said eagerly.

"'Oh no,' he said, 'Not so fast. Not before my wife gives birth to a boy. That was the deal.'

"I was really nervous now. What if she had a girl? No matter what he believed, I knew perfectly well that Jews are not sorcerers, and that his superstitions were utter nonsense. Believe me, at that moment I would have given anything to be a sorcerer and give the man his son on the spot. But fantasies are useless. I sat with him for two long, wearing hours, begging him to relinquish my niece, even though his wife had not yet given birth. He refused to budge. Then I had a brilliant idea. I told him that the only way I could promise that the baby would be a boy was if he would release Lenka to me at once. Otherwise, I would break the spell, and that would be the end of his son. G-d was with me, and he fell for it. I paid him the 30,000 zlotys which I always carried in my pocket - I guess magic only goes so far - and he handed Lenka over.

"She was sleeping, which was a good thing. I wrapped her in a blanket and brought her to my apartment. I couldn't close my eyes all night. Every few minutes I went over to check on her, to make sure she wasn't cold and was still breathing. That's how excited I was. I couldn't wait to see how happy she would be when she woke up in the morning. Again, I guess I really am naive, but I was sure that she had been waiting for this moment just as much as I had.

"The first five minutes shattered all my dreams. Lenka immediately recognized me as the man who had argued with her mother. She began to cry and stamp her feet. She refused to stop howling. `Mamma, save me! The Jew kidnapped me! Now he's going to kill me! Mamma, help me!' She kept it up nonstop.

"After several days of crying and screaming, she began to come to terms with the `kidnapping', and was willing to eat and drink. Throughout it all, she kept that miserable chain with the cross on it pressed tightly to her heart. She even talked to it, telling it that as soon as she could, she would run away back to Mamma, and tell her how the Jew had kidnapped her and wanted to kill her. And this was my sister Sara's daughter! I did my best to be patient with her. When she saw that I made no attempt to harm her, and in fact took good care of her, her attitude towards me changed somewhat, although even now, she's still suspicious. I've given the matter alot of thought, and I've come to the conclusion that I'm in no position to raise her or educate her, especially since I haven't given up on finding out if anyone else from our family survived. I plan to travel through Europe to search for them, and that's no life for a little girl."

He looked at his niece, who stood quietly behind him without saying a word. He stroked her hair gently; despite all the trouble she had given him, it was obvious that he still loved her very much. "I'm sure you understand, Rebbetzin," he said, "She needs warmth, understanding, and stability. She needs a normal life. I can't give her any of that right now. We have relatives in America, but I don't know enough about them to let her go them. I heard about Lidingo, and this is where I want her to be. I want her to be part of your family, to be educated the way your girls are."

He fell silent, but his eyes continued to plead with the Rebbetzin.

The Rebbetzin, who had listened wordlessly until then, looked from Avraham Levi to the cute little girl, and her heart broke. Finally she said, "I realize that you've gone through a great deal to get your niece back, but you have to understand that our girls are all teenagers. The classes and all the activities here are geared to that age group. What would a little girl like Lenka do here? Who would teach her, who would be her friends? Try to find another place, one with girls Lenka's age."

Lenka, the "little girl", among her older "sisters"

Mr. Levi was unmoved. He had made up his mind, and was not about to change it. "I realize that it won't be easy," he said, "But I want Lenka to be here. I've asked about the other schools in Sweden, and yours is the only one that's strictly orthodox. I want Lenka to be brought up as her parents would have wanted, without compromises."

"I'll have to consult with Mrs. Igell," said the Rebbetzin hesitantly. "If Lenka stays here, she'll be her responsibility."

Mrs. Igell immediately grasped just how very difficult it would be to accommodate Lenka in Lidingo, but she had a novel idea about how to deal with the problem. "Why don't we tell the girls about Lenka during supper? Let's hear what they think about having her stay in Lidingo," she suggested.

Mr. Levi and Lenka ate supper in the Rebbetzin's room. Mrs. Igell joined the girls in the dining room and asked for their attention. "Girls," she said calmly, "A little girl named Lenka has come to Lidingo. She's only four years old. We are not sure if she should stay, because we don't really have anyone here to look after her." Her eyes swept the dining room as she tried to gauge the girls' response before continuing. "Are any of you prepared to volunteer to be responsible for Lenka, like a mother?"

Esther was the first to raise her hand. All the other girls followed suit. Satisfied with the results of her experiment, Mrs. Igell brought Lenka into the dining room, where she was instantly surrounded by the Lidingo girls. They all wanted to see her, to touch her. What a treasure - a living Jewish child! The image of their own precious brothers and sisters, whom they would never see again, swam vividly before their eyes. Their love and longing for the missing children enveloped Lenka, making her their own.

Esther, now responsible for Lenka, sensed the little girl's distress, and announced that this was enough for now. "Can't you see how frightened she is, with so many people swarming over her all at once?" she said quietly. She smiled reassuringly at Lenka and took her hand. "Come, Lenka," she said, "I'll show you our room. It's time to get ready for bed."

When Lenka came to Lidingo, there were already about 120 girls there. There were eight to ten girls in a room, depending on the size of the room. Esther slept in one of the larger rooms. An eleventh bed was quickly procured and set up next to Esther's, complete with clean sheets and a pillow. Clothing was no problem; the big suitcase Lenka's uncle had brought along proved to be full of lovely new clothing he had bought for her before bringing her to Lidingo. Thanks to the love and understanding of her new sisters, Lenka was soon to become a Lidingo girl like all the rest.

The Mother of Lidingo

Everyone called her the "Rebbetzin". Something in this title attested to the boundless deference of the girls for this majestic figure who embodied so much for them. The great respect and esteem her personality commanded were not limited to her young students, or to the years she spent in Sweden. Wherever Rebbetzin Jacobson went, she radiated the nobility of refinement. She was a teacher par excellence, blessed with logic and intellect, whose every action lived up to her own high moral standards.

She was the rare type of woman who was serious and profound, and at the same time gentle and loving. None of her actions were left to chance. Her responses were weighed and reasoned, logical and carefully planned. Her natural intelligence was highlighted by wisdom born of fear of G-d. The depth of her emotion was often concealed, but it found its expression in her infinite devotion to the girls in Lidingo.

This noble woman put her devotion to the jewish people above her personal concerns. She devoted herself entirely to the Lidingo girls who so desperately needed her. It is amazing how Rebbetzin Jacobson, a young woman and mother, left her home and her little children in Stockholm, and went – at the urgent call of Rav Shlomo Wolbe – to lead Lidingo. She would go to Stockholm to see their children every week. On these weekly visits, the Rebbetzin would lavish love and attention on her sons and daughter, talking, listening, discussing, and offering advice and guidance. So powerful was the example of the Jacobsons that their children accepted their extended absences with good grace. They had absorbed enough of their parents' dedication to put the pain and loss of others above their own needs.

She was a mother to all. The Rebbetzin knew the pain and mental anguish of her daughters; it was she who understood their sorrow, no matter how it was expressed. She was attuned to the faintest signal of physical or emotional distress in her 120 girls. Years later, when the girls married and had children of their own, their "mother", the Rebbetzin, became a "grandmother", instructing, advising, and comforting her children. Bound by eternal ties of love, she continued to be there for them and their families, solving problems and looking out for their health and financial well-being as long as she lived.

However, perhaps the most precious gift the Rebbetzin gave her girls was their unparalleled fellowship, which lasted a lifetime. She imbued them with a rare sense of friendship and responsibility for one another. The girls went on to establish families all over the world, but even fifty years after leaving Lidingo they stay in touch, get together, and help each other in times of need: they are the Rebbetzin's "daughters".

By profession and personality, the Rebbetzin was an educator whose lessons became a legend. Those who attended felt they could never get enough. Her classes were not merely intellectual exercises in the transmission of information and the elegant resolution of difficulties in a text; they were a system for the development and enhancement of faith and awareness of G-d in the hearts of her students. The *Chumash* or *Tehillim* classes were vehicles to reawaken in the girls the world of values they had known at home, and from which they had been so brutally torn. She put no pressure on her students, allowing them to set their own pace of progress from *Rashi's* commentary on to those of *Malbim, Kli Yakar,* and more. In addition, from the springboard of class discussion, she subtly addressed each girl on a personal level, touching on the sensitive spots which needed attention without offending. Her classes nourished both the minds and the hearts of the girls, after years of intellectual and emotional deprivation.

The most amazing achievement of the Rebbetzin and the devoted Lidingo staff was their transformation of traumatized, brutalized orphans, broken in body and spirit, into lively, happy girls who went on to establish emotionally healthy families of their own, unscarred by the effects of the Holocaust. In later years, one of the Lidingo girls related that a friend of hers, a psychologist who had treated many Holocaust survivors, commented on her excellent mental health; she did not seem like a Holocaust survivor at all!

Lidingo's admission policy was quite liberal. Girls who had boarded with the family of a Christian minister in southern Sweden or with irreligious Jewish families, and sick girls recently discharged from non-kosher hospitals, all found a home in Lidingo. There were no preliminary requirements, and nothing was forced upon the girls. The educational framework and loving atmosphere exerted a subtle influence and inspiration on the girls for years to come to lead strictly orthodox homes.

A Lidingo graduate remembers:

"When I had children of my own, I always consulted with the Rebbetzin about their upbringing and education: what was the proper way to behave, to respond to daily challenges? She always gave me good advice. Once I told her that I had discovered a certain fault in one of my children.

"'What did you expect'?" the Rebbetzin said, 'Did you think you would give birth to angels?'

"Years later, the engagement of one of my children was celebrated outside of Jerusalem. As we approached the outskirts of the city, we passed the cemetery on *Har Hamenuchos*, where the Rebbetzin is buried. I found myself speaking to her silently, telling her my good news, sharing my happiness with her as if she were still alive. I have always felt her presence at joyous occasions in my family, even after she had passed away."

Another Lidingo girl describes the Rebbetzin's classes:

"The Rebbetzin did not lecture. Instead she guided us, until we arrived at the ideas she planned to pose on our own. She was totally involved in the topics she taught; even her face flushed with excitement. Her enthusiasm was contagious. It was as if *Rashi* himself was speaking to us through her. We didn't talk about `what is *Rashi's* question.' We talked about `what does *Rashi* want from us?' We learned in order to understand, remember, and do."

A pupil recalls:

"When the Rebbetzin wanted to cite a verse from *Tehillim*, but did not remember the exact quotation, I would help her, because I had a good memory. Before the war, I had memorized *Tehillim* by rote along with my brothers in *cheder*, but I still didn't understand any of it. My lack of comprehension mattered so much to the Rebbetzin that she found the time every morning before breakfast from 7:50 to 8:00, to tutor me privately in *Tehillim*, so that I learned to understand what I was saying."

Reminisces another girl:

"On the eve of Yom Kippur after lunch, before the *seudah mafsekes*, we all crowded into her room on the top floor to hear her speak about the Yom Kippur services in the Temple. The spiritual impact was enormous; I wish I could forgive my own children their minor transgressions today the way I forgave the entire Jewish people then."

The secret of the Rebbetzin's success as an educator lay in her own living example to the girls. Pola recalls just one of many instances from her time in Lidingo:

"The Rebbetzin never demanded anything of us that she did not demand of herself, that she did not personally fulfill. When visiting her and it was time for her to prepare supper for her husband, she invited us to join her in the kitchen, where she began her cooking. Once, after I was married, she came to visit me in my home. When she came in, she mentioned that she had to be home by 12:00, when the Rav arrived. Precisely at 11:40, she stood up to leave."

A former Lidingo girl tells the story of H.:

"One morning the Rebbetzin entered the classroom and found H., one of the best girls, reviewing her notes while the other girls ate breakfast in the dining room. The Rebbetzin's suspicions were immediately aroused, and she began to cross-examine H. Had she already eaten? Why wasn't she in the dining room with the others? At the Rebbetzin's prodding, H. was forced to disclose the truth. The question of how to express her thanks to the Al-mighty for having spared her from the Holocaust had troubled her greatly, until she hit upon what seemed to her to be the ideal solution: She would fast on Mondays and Thursdays. The Rebbetzin was horrified! In His weakened condition, such behavior was dangerous. She immediately arranged for Rav Jacobson, Rav Wolbe, and a third rav to meet in Lidingo and annul her vow. So vigilant was the Rebbetzin and so attuned to the girls' most subtle motivations, that she was able to intervene before any damage was done."

The Rebbetzin remained in constant contact with Rav Wolbe throughout the years in Lidingo. It was she who directed the institution and mothered the girls, for whose benefit no sacrifice was too great. Nevertheless, she would not make a move without consulting him and receiving his blessing.

The Lidingo girls, regardless of their backgrounds, remained Torah observant even after they left the Rebbetzin's constant instruction. This is a tribute to her unique personality and selfless dedication to them all.

The Father of the "Angels"

The Rebbetzin combined a very exalted personality with down-to-earth practicality. Her husband, Rav Jacobson, on the other hand, was entirely different, all emotion and fervor. Nothing was too difficult for the Rav when it came to bringing joy to the girls. If one of them was unhappy, he would coax a smile to her face with a witticism or a joke. To restore their *joie de vivre*, he was not above telling amusing stories or composing impromptu rhymes. Despite the heavy and by no means humorous burden of keeping Lidingo afloat, he made himself personally responsible for boosting the girls' morale. No matter how busy he was, Rav Jacobson always found the time to say the right thing at the right moment to a dejected girl, restoring feelings of self esteem and self-respect destroyed by years of humiliation in the camps.

Travel, whether by air, sea, or land, was no simple matter in the post-war years. It was neither safe nor easy. Yet in order to keep Lidingo going, Rav Jacobson made many arduous trips, both in Sweden and abroad. Regardless of the strains involved in these frequent traveling, back in Lidingo, the girls always found him happy and easygoing, with a special smile for every one of his "angels," as he called them.

With all their strikingly different personalities, the Rav and the Rebbetzin worked together as a unit, forming a unified whole. For example, while the Rebbetzin's restraint and refinement were essential to the educational structure of Lidingo, it was the Rav who swept the girls along in the fiery enthusiasm of his *Shabbos* evening talks, making them wonderful, unforgettable experiences. He always began in exactly the same way: *Meine liebe kinder* - my beloved children...

One of the Lidingo girls recalls:

"Why was it that every time the Rav looked at us his eyes would fill with tears, even while his face was wreathed in his ever-present warm-hearted smile, and while he was telling us such clever jokes? What was the meaning of these tears? Were they tears of sorrow for us weak, lonely girls, firebrands saved from the fire, but scorched, inside and out, nonetheless? Were they tears of fear and uncertainty over the future of so many young orphans, bereft of spiritual stamina? Were they tears of mourning for the six million precious brothers and sisters, men and women, old and young, who were killed to sanctify G-d's Name? They were all of these, and more. These were not tears shed once to relieve the pain and allow him to go on; they were fresh and new every time he saw us. His compassionate heart refused to be consoled over the tragedy which had befallen his people.

"Rav Jacobson saw in each of the Lidingo girls the sole survivor of an illustrious family from a town or village in Poland, Germany, Hungary, Czechoslovakia, Roumania, or Lithuania. He sought the positive in each of us and strove to make the others see it too. One girl had unique talents, another had wonderful character traits, a third had a phenomenal memory, yet another had unblemished fear of Heaven: in Rav Jacobson's eyes, we were all special, beloved members of the Jewish people. He searched our family trees for prestigious lineage, when he found that one of us had renowned ancestors, his joy knew no bounds. He used the information to raise our self-esteem and lift us from the profound depression from which many of us suffered. If facts were unavailable, Rav Jacobson simply made them up, believing that all Israel is of distinguished lineage, even if we don't know the details.

"As much as we loved it, we had to admit that sometimes he was excessive in the praises he conjured up. But Rav Jacobson nevertheless consistently practiced his educational policy: he really believed that students are as good as they are thought to be. He was always encouraging us and trying to make us happy. Before difficult tests, he did his best to see to it that we did not feel worried or pressured."

Many of the girls in Lidingo arrived there as a result of Rav Jacobson's personal efforts. He traveled the length and breadth of Sweden, again and again, sparing no hardship, searching the refugee camps for one more Jewish girl who could be saved from assimilation and be returned to her people. There were no Jewish communities in these distant regions and no facilities for kosher food, but a Jewish girl's future was more important to him than his own comfort. His perception of his work as a sacred task gave him the strength to go on, and G-d blessed him with success. In Lidingo, his classes on Jewish law opened new vistas for the girls, many of whom were confused about the fundamentals of Judaism, and taught them how to live new, meaningful lives.

For the girls he symbolized the unforgettable home, the father and the *zeidy*, their home and their lost family.

Chava relates: "I will never forget my first visit to the Rav's home in Stockholm after the war. A friend and I had come from the hospital to spend a holiday with a Jewish family. When we came in, I saw a woman with her head covered and a tall, bearded man sitting and learning Torah. Behind him was a big bookcase filled with religious books. Without thinking, I blurted out, `*Oy, a seforim shafeh*, just like at home!' It had been so long since I'd seen a bearded Jew, and the sight of the Rav brought back my own home."

Life in post-war Sweden was not easy for a religious Jewish family. The Jacobson residence in Stockholm was an island of sanctity and spiritual elevation in a sea of assimilation and alienation from all things Jewish. This private home became public property, serving as a de facto kosher restaurant for any Jew passing through Stockholm and in need of a kosher meal.

In retrospect, the girls agree that these two diverse personalities, the Rav and the Rebbetzin, were essential to Lidingo. Their impact on their young students was vital and unforgettable.

The First Shabbos

Everyone in Lidingo, students and staff, dressed in their Shabbos best, had assembled in the Green Hall (named for its green painted walls), ready to receive the Shabbos Queen. Their faces shone as they joined, relaxed and united, in singing *Lecha Dodi*. These were beautiful moments at the end of a busy week.

Chava remembers her first Shabbos in Lidingo, shortly before *Pesach*, 1946, as an overwhelmingly emotional experience.

A survivor of Auschwitz and Bergen-Belsen, Chava had suffered from almost total physical debilitation, and was brought to Sweden to recuperate in a hospital near Stockholm. Like the other refugee girls, she had distrusted the hospital staff, despite their obvious concern. To the bafflement and anger of the nurses, the girls had persisted in hiding slices of bread under their pillows. The nurses simply could not understand their insistent explanations that they had to hide the bread, in case there would not be another meal.

A Hungarian Jew named Reb Gross, a wonderful man with a small beard and a big heart, was making the rounds of the Swedish hospitals, looking for Hungarian Jews in need of assistance. When he met Chava and her friends in the hospital, he told them about a new, strictly orthodox school in a place called Lidingo. Chava, who had never really expected to see another Jew again, was thrilled. She, together with a number of other Hungarian girls, formed the school's "Hungarian group."

After prayers in the Green Hall, they all went to the dining room. For the first time since she had been taken from her home, Chava saw *Shabbos* candles. The tables, arranged in a U, were set with clean white tablecloths and real china. Looking back now, Chava remembered the sweet feeling of warmth and belonging which had enveloped her as she joined hands with the other girls, dancing along with them as they sang *Shalom Aleichem*. Their spirits soared as they were caught up in the dance, their young voices singing a song of greeting to G-d's heavenly angels. Chava could almost picture these angels spreading their wings over the old, run-down building, bestowing Heaven's blessing on a group of orphaned Jewish girls.

That night was also the first time she had heard Rav Jacobson speak, expounding on that week's Torah reading. It was then that she felt the warmth he generated, as she listened eagerly to the affectionate, encouraging words he showered on them as he spoke. On that first *Shabbos*, listening to the Rav, Chava understood that she had gained something priceless by coming to Lidingo. It was only later that she would learn that the sincere, selfless concern Rav Jacobson so freely expressed in his talks was the secret of his greatness.

Bikur Cholim

Bikur cholim was an unavoidable fact of life for the girls in Lidingo.

There were still many girls who had not yet recovered from the ordeal of the Holocaust. Some had contracted tuberculosis, while others were in a state of total physical exhaustion. Some of the girls had suffered damage to their nervous systems, and their weakened bodies had not yet begun to function normally. Unfortunately, some of the girls were still in isolation and unable to have visitors. They were very, very ill, and their lives hung by a thread; others, returned their pure souls to their *Maker* in Swedish hospitals, despite sincere efforts by the excellent Swedish doctors and the dedicated nurses to save them. The ugly hand of the Nazi monster continued to do its work even after its victims had escaped its reach.

These sick girls and women thirsted for words of comfort and solace, for warm words of hope. These and more were bestowed lovingly and generously by the kindhearted girls from Lidingo, who knew many of the patients personally. They felt a profound emotional need to help their friends. Who knew as well as they what these girls had endured, and who could do a better job of comforting their troubled souls?

The *bikur cholim* project was the product of the girls' own initiative and organization, and the Lidingo staff was all for it. The doctors and nurses welcomed the visits for their therapeutic effect on the patients.

Every two weeks the Lidingo girls would receive an allowance of five Swedish *kronor*. From this modest sum, they scrupulously set aside ten percent for charity. With the money thus accumulated, they purchased flour, sugar, cocoa, eggs, and other ingredients for baking. When the cooks would leave for the day, the girls took over the kitchen, trying their hand at producing the greatest possible variety of pastries with the limited ingredients at their disposal.

Armed with cakes and cookies, as well as oranges, dates, candy, and whatever other small gifts they could obtain for their friends, they took turns making the rounds of the hospitals. This *mitzvah* was far from an easy one in those days. While one of the hospitals they visited was near Stockholm, the others were in Uttran and Arla, several hours away from Lidingo. Most girls traveled through the night, so that they would have a full day to spend with the patients. At the hospital, the girls would split up and head for different wards, where they distributed the sweets, freshly baked cakes and cookies, and other little surprises.

At first, one or two members of the staff would accompany the girls on these trips. '*Morah*' Chaya, with her vibrant personality, energy, and determination was a real asset on these occasions. She threw herself wholeheartedly into the task of cheering up the sick girls, talking, joking, playing games, and singing. She would seat the stronger girls on chairs in the wide hospital corridors, while the weaker ones watched and listened from their rooms. Chaya would tell stories and lead them in familiar, beloved songs from the past. Caught in her spell, the girls joined in happily. On one memorable occasion, the chairs were occupied by Leah from Ravensbruck, Esther from Auschwitz, and Bracha from Bergen-Belsen, as well as girls from other camps, whose survival was nothing short of miraculous. While they had not forgotten the horrors they had witnessed and endured, they were buoyed by the sight of the Lidingo girls, who had suffered like them but were cheerful and smiling nonetheless. Perhaps, they dared to hope, they too would smile again some day...

"All together now," Chaya called out, "*Hinei ma tov uma naim, sheves achim gam yachad* (how pleasant it is for brothers to sit together)," she sang.

The girls could not match her gusto, but the joy and thanks in their eyes spoke louder than words. One song led to another. Sorke, Rivka, and Brachie from Lidingo were there too, contributing to the joyous mood in the dismal hospital hallway. Suddenly, a loud cry interrupted the singing.

"Chaya! Chaya! It's me - Dina Melamed from Stutthof. Don't you remember me?"

Chaya froze, unable to believe her ears and her eyes. She craned her neck and saw Dinush, little Dinush from Stutthof. How could she ever forget her? Chaya had been sure she would never see her again. Dina was in isolation, so Chaya had to restrain her urge to embrace her.

Chaya pulled herself together. "Dinush!" she cried, "What a wonderful surprise to see you here!" She had many questions, but was too overwhelmed by her tears and her memories to say any more. Dinush...

* * *

The barracks in the Stutthof concentration camp were packed with helpless typhus victims awaiting their turn in the gas chambers. Stuffed like sardines into dirty three tiered bunks, many succumbed to starvation and the ravages of their illness even before their numbers were called. One terrible night, Chaya, too sick to hold her head up, heard crying from the bunk underneath hers. She knew it was inhabited by Mrs. Melamed and her twelve-year-old daughter Dina, both of whom were very sick. However, bowed by disease, despair, and the stark knowledge of their inevitable fate, they had barely spoken. Why were they crying now? What had happened?

"Mrs. Melamed?" she croaked, "Is that you? Why are you crying?"

"It's me, Dinush," came the choked reply.

"Dinush? Why are you crying?"

Dina broke down completely. "My mother," she wept, "She's dead."

"*Baruch Dayan Emes,*" Chaya said softly. These words, uttered at the news of a death, were repeated constantly in the camps. Yet deep in her heart, Chaya envied Mrs. Melamed: she would suffer no more.

"What will happen to me now?" cried Dinush, "I have no one left in the whole world! I want to die too!" she moaned.

"G-d forbid, Dinush," said Chaya, "You are not alone and you are not going to die. Here, climb up to my bunk." She helped Dina up and put her thin arms around her. "Dinush," she told her, "From now on, you are my sister. We'll go everywhere together, and I'll take care of you. Don't worry, G-d will help us, you'll see."

Slowly, Dinush's crying ceased. She clung tightly to Chaya. She fell asleep, still moaning, "Mamma, my Mamma."

Chaya had been unable to prevent their eventual separation, and she'd had no idea that the delicate young girl was still alive, until their unexpected meeting in a Swedish hospital.

* * *

The month of *Kislev* arrived, and everyone in Lidingo was busy with preparations for the first Chanukah after the war. Under Chaya's direction, the girls produced a play and a concert. Despite their own excitement, they did not forget their friends in the hospitals, and kept up their scheduled visits as always. It was Etika's turn to go to the hospital in Uttran. She and her friends spent the night before her trip in the kitchen, baking delicious cakes for the sick girls. Etika also took along a letter for each girl. She knew them all and felt close to each of them, but she felt a special bond to eighteen-year-old Sorke. Not only had Sorke spent an entire year together with Etika in the camps, she had also literally saved Etika's life.

* * *

Etika was in the youth barracks in Auschwitz, the one designated for girls between the ages of twelve and sixteen. Occasionally younger girls, who looked older than their years, managed to sneak into this barracks. Unfortunately, although Etika was thirteen, she was small and thin, which made her the constant victim of the kapo's sadism. But Etika, mentally and emotionally was far too mature for her years, proved herself useful and was allowed to stay.

When Etika's transport had arrived in Auschwitz, she'd had no idea of where she was. Everything happened with dizzying speed. Before she even had a chance to look around, she found herself thrust into line, marching five abreast across the square to some unknown destination. At least she had her younger sister at her side.

As they marched, she noticed women with shaved heads peering out of the barracks along the camp paths. How awful, she thought, and shuddered. When the women saw the newcomers, they shouted, "Do you have any bread? Give it to us. They're going to take away everything anyway, so you might as well give us the bread."

Etika looked at them pityingly. Poor things, they must be insane. Why else would they be locked up in those barracks with their heads shaved? But why were they begging for bread? Wasn't there any food here? It couldn't be that they really had to beg. They had to be mad! Why, just look at the fat woman guarding them, lashing out again and again with her whip. She looked cruel and the women cringed, but Etika figured that perhaps they were violent, difficult to control.

All too soon, Etika would learn where she was and understand what she had seen. Everything happened with the same brutal speed. There was no time to think or question. They were ordered to remove the clothes they had brought from home and were given other clothing. Small girls were given large uniforms, while the bigger ones were purposely given clothes too small for them. As if that was not bad enough, their hair was then unceremoniously shorn: now they too were bald. In minutes, they had been transformed beyond recognition into miserable, debased slaves.

Etika looked at the women and girls around her. For a moment, she thought that they were the women she had seen in the barracks. Then she understood... it seemed that in Auschwitz, everyone was insane.

As long as she lived, Etika would never forget the hours she and her fellow prisoners had spent standing on their feet with both hands raised, from the cold of pre-dawn to the heat of midday. The sting of the whip on those too "lazy" to keep their hands elevated and immobile for hours, the meager portions of moldy bread, the tormenting hunger and never ending thirst, were all indelibly engraved in her memory. She was only thirteen years old.

In the barracks, close to one thousand girls lay jammed together on the wooden bunks, too tightly packed to move. In response to a pre-arranged signal, they all turned over together, when one side grew sore from the pressure. How ironic, she often thought, that it was in Auschwitz that pampered Etika had learned to cook and bake. Gripped by hunger, the girls would huddle together and longingly recall the recipes for delicacies their mothers had made at home.

One day the rumor spread through the camp that the dreaded murderer Mengele was going to pay them a visit. Curfew was imposed. By now, everyone knew what that meant: a selection.

The girls in the barracks were terrified. They had heard that Mengele, a physician by profession, conducted horrendous experiments on the Jewish women in the camps. What could they do to save themselves from his clutches? There was no way of knowing whom he would choose, but Etika was afraid that being so small and thin, she was useless for hard labor, but definitely good enough for experiments.

Etika grabbed her younger sister and ran with her to the main toilets, where she hoped they could hide, unnoticed. They found many other women there who had had the same idea. Their hearts pounded painfully as they waited for the signal that the selection was over. When they returned to the barracks, they were horrified to find that of the thousand girls they had left behind, only three hundred had - for the moment - escaped Mengele. Their relief at their salvation was short-lived. Within minutes, an immediate second selection was announced; the Germans had realized that some of the women were hiding, and they did not plan to let them off so easily.

Etika did not know what to do. Confusion and a fierce desire to live propelled her towards the outer edge of the camp. Panting from the exertion, she looked up and saw an SS guard pointing his gun at her. Without a word, she dragged her trembling body back in the direction of the barracks.

"Oh G-d," she said silently, "I am Your lamb and You are my Shepherd. You decide."

The soldier kept his gun trained on Etika, but for some reason, he did not shoot. From a distance, she saw that the second selection was already being conducted in her barracks. To return now was suicide. But where could she go?

That was when Sorke, an older teenager from the women's barracks, came to her aid. "Psst... psst..." she hissed, "Come here, quick!"

Etika ran to the women's barracks. Sorke and her comrades shoved the skinny girl under the bottom bunk. Then they sat down on the bunk, concealing her with their feet. When the SS guards came looking for her, Sorke vehemently denied that the girl had come anywhere near the women's barracks. She was so confident and persuasive that they actually believed her. Late that night, Etika sneaked back into the girls' barracks. Her friends were thrilled to see her alive, and Etika thanked her Creator; the Shepherd had watched over His lamb.

But Etika's joy soon turned to grief. Her sister, who had been with her from the start, was gone, and Etika knew she would never see her again. Her spirits fell, and only the knowledge that Sorke, her savior, was still alive provided her with some degree of consolation. During roll call, Etika would stealthily check to make sure Sorke was still standing with the others. Sorke would shoot her a quick, furtive glance, their signal that all was well, and that Etika should continue to be strong. These seconds kept Etika going until the girls were transferred out of Auschwitz and separated. There was no way for either of them to know where the other was, or what fate had befallen her.

* * *

Sorke had survived. Etika found her lying in a hospital bed, dying of tuberculosis. Her lovely black hair had begun to grow in after the last shaving in camp, but it lacked healthy body and shape. Sorke's big dark eyes were open wide, as if to devour all the sights before her, but they revealed nothing. Her arms hung limply at her side, almost as if they weren't really hers. She was on an intravenous drip, and an oxygen tank was kept ready at her bed at all times. The nurses would tiptoe into Sorke's room, trying to hide their concern as they checked on her condition and did their best to make her comfortable. Sorke was apathetic, totally detached from her surroundings. No one knew what she was experiencing; all attempts to get her to talk were fruitless.

Every day in her prayers, Etika would ask that Sorke be healed, along with all the sick of Israel. How could she forget Sorke, who had hidden her during the selection and saved her life? Her room was always Etika's first stop on her visits to Uttran.

Etika knocked on Sorke's door, but the older girl did not even turn her head in response. Etika did not wait for an invitation. She was the only one who could get Sorke to open her mouth, and she saw the glimmer of interest in Sorke's eyes as she approached her bed.

"How are you today, Sorke dear?" Etika tried to put a happy lilt in her voice. "Here, I brought you something - letters from all the girls. Everyone is very worried about you."

Sorke did not respond. Her dull eyes expressed deep sadness. Etika took her cold hand in her own and hugged her tenderly. "Oh, my Sorke, won't you tell me how you feel?" she said.

"*Baruch Hashem.*" Always the same question, and always the same answer.

"You look much better," Etika lied. "You see? With G-d's help, you will get better. Just have a bit more patience and everything will pass, as if it never happened."

"No, Etika," said Sorke quietly, "Not this time. I've cheated death many times, but now I know, I feel, that this is it. Maybe it's better this way..."

"Sorke, don't talk like that! I don't care what you feel, this time you're wrong!" cried Etika from the depths of her soul. "Just look at Rocheleh and Tova and Penina. They were just as sick as you, and now they're fine, with G-d's help. Even Dinush will be in Lidingo soon, and so will you! Don't ever talk like that again."

Sorke smiled weakly at her young friend. "What are you getting so worked up about, Etika?" she whispered, "That's the way of the world. Everyone gets there sometime. This world is a big, beautiful corridor, but the banquet hall is even more beautiful." She stared at the ceiling, Etika apparently forgotten. "The question is, how will we arrive, with what baggage..." Suddenly, she turned to Etika and smiled, a real smile this time. "It's so strange. Every time I was near death, I would picture how it would finally happen. Once I decided that it would be the gas chambers. Another time I was sure I would be shot. Once I could even see myself digging a mass grave with all the others. After we finished digging, the Germans would shoot us and it would all be over. But I never imagined I would die like this, in a clean bed, with the war over and done with."

"Enough!" screamed Etika, "I don't want to hear another word! With G-d's help, you are going to live for years and years! Do you hear me? Years! You went through it all, Sorke, you saved my life, you helped everyone, and your merits will sustain you."

"Every person is allotted his own number of years," said Sorke. "Why do you think I was granted the privilege of dying quietly in bed, and not in some horrible way like our other brothers and sisters? It can only be my own few merits, and the merits of my saintly fathers, whose blood saturated the earth. I thank G-d that I've been allowed this time to repent and come closer to my Creator before I die."

Etika paled. Every time this conversation of theirs was repeated, all her entreaties to Sorke to stop were of no avail. It seemed as if Sorke had risen above life in this world. Etika had discussed it with the Rebbetzin after her last visit. The Rebbetzin had reassured her, explaining that apparently Sorke had achieved a very high level of closeness to G-d.

To Etika's relief, Sorke finally changed the subject. "Have you found anyone yet?" she asked.

"No, not yet, but I haven't stopped looking," Etika replied.

"Don't give up hope, Etika, you can never tell. But you know what? To me, it doesn't really matter if I meet them here or there. The main thing is that we meet again. I have a feeling that it won't be long," she added dreamily.

Before Etika could answer, Sorke changed the subject yet again. "They're so wonderful to me here - the doctors, the nurses, everyone. Look what a nice room I have, just for me."

It was obvious that the conversation was tiring Sorke, and Etika realized that it was time to go. It was hard for her to leave Sorke like this. She knew all too well that she was the only one to whom Sorke bared her soul. As for Etika herself, she had not found a single living member of her family, and Sorke was like a sister to her, the only one she had left. Despite the seriousness of her condition, Etika refused to believe that Sorke might not make it. She prayed for her recovery, clinging desperately to any shred of hope.

When she left Sorke's room, Etika put a smile on her face, not wanting the other patients to sense her worry. She was here to cheer them, not depress them. She began to make the rounds, stopping at each bed, asking the girls how they felt, and handing out the letters and parcels from Lidingo. Troubled as she was about Sorke, their joy and gratitude comforted her.

Today it was Etika's turn to show them they were not forgotten by their more fortunate friends, who eagerly awaited their arrival in Lidingo. Next time, Tzilinka or Leah or Rochke would come, bearing the same message of hope.

The Chanukah Party

When Etika returned to Lidingo, she was both physically and emotionally drained. All she wanted was to go to bed and sleep. But time had not stood still in Lidingo. An atmosphere of gaiety and anticipation pervaded the campus. Preparations for the Chanukah party were well underway, and instead of the longed for quiet, Etika found barely suppressed pandemonium. In one corner girls were practicing their lines for the play. In another, they were having choir practice. Wherever she went, girls were busy with decorations, refreshments, and other vital necessities. No one wanted to be left out.

One matter which was not discussed until the very last minute was the actual lighting of the Chanukah candles. This was the first Chanukah after the war, and no one knew where the candles would be lit, or whether they would be of oil or wax. No one dared ask the most obvious, and most awful, question: who would light the candles? The staff realized that this was a sensitive subject, and they said nothing.

Erev Chanukah arrived, bringing with it a frenzy of last minute preparation. The entire building was festooned with decorations, and the dining room tables were laden with homemade *latkes*, filling the room with their own special fragrance. Everyone waited for Rav Jacobson to arrive and signal the start of the festivities. With his affability and special sense of humor, he was always able to generate just the right atmosphere on every occasion.

With a broad smile on his face, the Rav entered the dining room, accompanied by the guests who had come especially to Lidingo for the party. The effect was electric. The Rav sensed the girls' tension, and his smile broadened even more as he looked lovingly at them all. He approached the menorah, and in his beautiful voice, pronounced the blessings over the wax candles. The girls' "Amen" was louder than usual; it was almost impossible for them to control their emotions. Where had they been last Chanukah? Who had lit Chanukah candles then?

The guests, including representatives of the Swedish Ministry of Education, distinguished members of the Stockholm community, and many others, were overwhelmed as the girls began to sing *Maoz Tzur*. The speeches they made later were full of praise for the students and staff.

This was not the Ministry of Education's first encounter with Lidingo. After the school's opening, Dr. Ehrenpreis, head of the Stockholm reform community, had complained that it was functioning poorly and ought to be closed. A government committee of inquiry had arrived shortly afterwards. They were so favorably impressed by the school's academic level, student performance, and efficient management that Sweden's Minister of Education had taken the trouble to send a personal letter of commendation. Lidingo, despite the slurs of its detractors, had already gained a reputation as the leading institution of its kind in Sweden. Now, in a private Chanukah miracle, instead of withdrawing its support from Lidingo, the government increased it!

Next on the agenda was the Lidingo choir, singing the school anthem. '*Morah*' Chaya led the girls in the Hebrew songs, while Mr. Igell, the school's administrator, provided a simultaneous translation into Swedish. Dressed in identical outfits, the girls sang heartily.

Bais Yaakov is our school,
There we learn Torah,
We aspire to go to our Land,
For from Zion shall go forth Torah.

The teachers instruct us,
In the study of Torah and the holy tongue,
They enlighten us
About the holiness of G-d and His commandments.

We observe the *mitzvos* of our Torah,
And fulfill the word of G-d,
When we reach our Land
We will keep them there as G-d commands.

Next came a dramatization of the Chanukah lights, represented by nine girls wrapped in white sheets and crowned with torches. Each light presented itself and told its story. The rest of the girls had heard them practice their lines so often that they unconsciously mouthed them along with the performers.

Then Chaya announced the Chanukah play, inviting the actresses onstage by name. She told the story of Chanukah in rhymed couplets, as the girls portrayed Antiochus, Yehudis, and Helifornes. They depicted the Jews' battle to observe the Torah despite all obstacles. It was a moving and convincing presentation.

Concluding the program was the choir's rendition of a medley of songs about *Eretz Yisrael*, where the girls hoped to live one day.

And then - it was over. The girls quickly cleared the dining room and hurried to their rooms, where they could give free reign to the choking tears which had threatened to burst forth during the party. They wept for their fathers, who had lit Chanukah candles of pure olive oil in their own beautiful menorahs; for their mothers, who had prepared the best *latkes* in the world; for their brothers and sisters with whom they had sung *Maoz Tzur*; for the family togetherness of shared games, sweets, and surprises, lost to them forever. They remembered, and cried bitter tears for their murdered loved ones who had struggled under inhuman conditions to fulfill G-d's commandments until they too were consumed by the flames. It was Chanukah, but they could never forget.

Thirst

The girls in Lidingo were eager to study - sometimes too eager. Their thirst for knowledge bordered on addiction. Every free moment was used for study, even to the point of breaking the rules. It was an ironclad policy of the Rebbetzin's that lights-out was at 11:00 P.M., and wake up at 7:00 A.M. to give the girls a good eight hours sleep. She stressed repeatedly that sleep was no less important in the maintenance of a healthy body than nourishing food. When the Rebbetzin found overly diligent girls poring over their books in the wee hours of the morning, she was very angry. Understanding as she was, this was one thing she would not tolerate.

One night, the Rebbetzin and Mrs. Igell were up very late discussing some urgent matters that had come up in Lidingo. When the Rebbetzin left the Igells' apartment, she passed the girls' rooms, and saw that some of them were still up studying. She didn't say anything, but the disapproval on her face was obvious.

In the next day's class, she wove her opinion of the girls' actions into her discussion of the Torah commentaries. She did not digress from the subject matter, but she made the point that there is a time and a place for everything, including a time for study and a time for rest. She emphasized that not only were the girls depriving themselves of much needed sleep, they were also stealing sleep from their roommates by keeping the lights on late at night. The situation improved considerably after that. But, there are exceptions to every rule...

* * *

"Nechama, are you asleep yet?" Matti whispered as she crept into their room. It was 1:00 A.M., and even the most studious girls were already in bed.

"No, I can't fall asleep," Nechama whispered back. She sat up in bed and rubbed her tired eyes. "Why do you study so late?" she asked Matti. "You know how angry the Rebbetzin gets when girls stay up after eleven."

Matti did not answer. She turned away and began to make up her bed, hiding her flushed, saddened face from her roommate.

Nechama watched Matti. "You're acting awfully strange today," she commented. "What happened?"

"What you said would happen," was Matti's cryptic reply.

"What I said about what?"

"About the Rebbetzin being angry when the girls stay up late." It was obvious that she found it very difficult to talk. "I - I was punished by the Rebbetzin. I can't come to her class tomorrow," she said in a forlorn, miserable voice.

Nechama was very disturbed. Missing the Rebbetzin's class was an irretrievable loss. No matter how hard one tried to copy notes and make up the missed material, there was no substitute for hearing the Rebbetzin's own delivery.

"The Rebbetzin came up to check if everyone was asleep," Matti said, "She found me sitting with my books. Everyone had already gone to sleep, but I wanted to review my notes one last time before class. You know, she was really, really angry at me. She said we don't understand that sleep is just as important for us as food, and certainly more important than study. She also said that we can't possibly gain anything from what we learn, or apply it, if we don't take care of our health."

"She's right," Nechama said thoughtfully. While Matti couldn't be excused from the Rebbetzin's punishment, she hoped that at least she would learn her lesson.

"Of course the Rebbetzin's right," Matti agreed, "But I can't stop myself. Nechama, you don't know how we missed school all those years in the camps. As awful as it was, we never lost our thirst to learn. We lived in the shadow of the crematoria, and dreamed of going back to school," Matti said wistfully. "And now, with G-d's help, we're here, and we're learning, not just in school, but with Rebbetzin Jacobson. Each of her classes is an education in itself." Forgetting the sleeping girls around her, her voice rose sharply. "Don't you understand? I just can't get enough! I can't stop! I want to learn and learn, to make up for everything I lost..." She covered her face with her hands, and her voice dropped to a whisper. "And now the Rebbetzin is angry with me. What shall I do?"

"Do what the Rebbetzin says. Go to bed on time, and keep your studying for the daytime," Nechama replied practically.

To tell the truth, Matti's unquenchable thirst for knowledge was foreign to her. She enjoyed her schoolwork, as they all did, but she enjoyed many other activities as well. When her homework was done, she spent her spare time singing, dancing, sketching, or just chatting comfortably with her friends. But she was wise enough to recognize that everyone is different, and she respected her friend's right to be herself.

Matti sank down on her bed. "I don't really have any choice. I'll just have to miss the Rebbetzin's class this one time. I was always afraid of this happening; when Itta and Sara were punished, I prayed that I wouldn't be caught, and not have to miss a class. But I broke the rules, and now I have to pay the price."

* * *

Matti's thoughts wandered to the not-so-distant past. Vivid pictures flashed through her mind. She saw herself, an innocent little eight-year-old on her way to school, schoolbag in hand, proudly wearing her school uniform. All of her books and notebooks were neatly covered, and all her homework was done. She had been so happy... She also remembered the gentile children who would appear out of nowhere, pelting her with stones and shouting curses at her and at Jews in general.

That had only been the beginning. It soon became too dangerous for Matti to go out alone. Her father had passed away several years earlier, so an older cousin began to accompany her to school and back. Soon it got worse. Jews were forbidden to walk on the sidewalks; they would have to take their chances dodging traffic in the street. Then came the yellow star, turning the Jews into easy targets for any passing Pole. Beatings of Jews on the city streets in broad daylight became commonplace, but no one dared to raise his voice in protest. The Jews were terrorized and defenseless. All they could do was hope and pray that

The "yellow star"

the madness would pass, that the government would come to their defense and curb the excesses. It didn't happen.

The next stop was the ghetto. Matti's family left their comfortable, spacious home with its beautiful furnishings behind, and began their lives in the ghetto with only a few essential belongings. They all moved into a small apartment, shared with her grandmother, uncles, aunts, cousins, and, unbelievably, several additional families. They were always hungry, and no one had any idea of what the next day would bring. Yet still Matti and her contemporaries went to school, now in the ghetto, studying hard and doing homework conscientiously. Despite the terrible sadness in their eyes, Matti's mother and grandmother tried hard to maintain a pleasant atmosphere at home.

Frightening rumors abounded in the ghetto about the German atrocities perpetrated on Jews, with the enthusiastic assistance of the Polish populace. It was said that Jews were being sent to concentration camps, where they were killed in horrible ways. Could it be true? How could it be true? As much as they did not want to believe what they heard, fear and doubt gnawed at the hearts of the Jews trapped in the ghetto.

Matti's uncle Shmelke lived in Radom. He was one of the few lucky ones: he performed "essential services" for the Germans, and thus had "good papers" which provided him with not only a measure of protection and preferential treatment, but also the priceless bonus of permission to live outside the ghetto. He too heard the rumors of the terrible fate awaiting the Jews in the ghettos, and after weighing the options, he decided that Matti, at least, could be saved. For a small fortune, a gentile woman agreed to take the risk of smuggling Matti out of the ghetto in her hometown and bringing her to uncle Shmelke in Radom.

The woman examined Matti critically, and it was obvious that she was displeased. "You look too Jewish," she said flatly.

The terrified little girl understood that it was not a good thing to look Jewish, but what could she do?

The woman tied an ugly peasant handkerchief tightly around Matti's head, covering much of her face. "This stays on your head at all times," she ordered as she tightened the knot under Matti's chin. "You have a terrible toothache, understand?"

Matti nodded her head, too frightened and confused to argue. After a tearful parting from her mother, she set out for the railroad station with the gentile woman. A clumsy coat hung from her shoulders, and the handkerchief covered most of her face.

As they prepared to board the train, the woman told her, "Look out the window until we get to Radom, so that no one will see your face and realize that you're Jewish."

Matti dutifully glued her face to the dirty window, watching the endless green fields, crowned with colorful wreaths of flowers. In the distance, she could see the mountains surrounding the fields, as if to protect them. Leafy trees waved their branches peacefully. The bright spring sun shone benevolently over the entire scene, and Matti felt that it shone for her too, Jewess though she was. Looking out the window wasn't hard at all. Everything was going to be just fine.

A scream shattered Matti's serenity. "Look! A Jewess! I swear it, that girl has got to be a Jewess!"

A Jewess! The entire car was in an uproar. Everyone was on their feet, staring, examining, and cursing. But Matti's guardian was not so easily daunted.

"What do you mean, a Jewess?" she protested, "What nonsense! This is my daughter, Maria." She drew Matti close and hugged her. "Poor thing, she's got a terrible toothache. You should be ashamed of yourselves, frightening an innocent child like that. She's terrified of Jews." She carefully gauged the mood of the crowd. Seeing that they believed her, she boldly added, "I don't envy you if you frighten my Maria again. I'll call the police, and then we'll see who's smart."

The other passengers, rather embarrassed by her daring, left them alone. Slowly, their racing hearts slowed down to normal. Matti turned her unseeing eyes to the window and prayed. The rest of the trip passed uneventfully. When Shmelke saw his little niece and heard about the close call on the train, he thanked G-d, and sat down to plan the next step.

It was clear to Uncle Shmelke that Matti, with her typically Jewish features, could not pass as an Aryan on a regular basis. Her escape from the crowd on the train was a miracle, and miracles do not happen every day. If Matti was to remain outside the ghetto, she would have to stay indoors. For a time this was enough, but when the danger worsened, Shmelke was forced to entrust her to her aunts in the ghetto for the night. Thus Matti spent her days cowering alone in her uncle's apartment on the Aryan side, and her nights shivering in fear with the Jews in the ghetto. It was only a question of time before Radom's Jews were deported. Thanks to Shmelke's foresight, Matti was spared this fate, at least for the time being.

In exchange for a huge bribe, Matti was placed in the home of a non-Jewish family. Locked in their attic, unable to see the light of day or to breathe fresh air, she spent her days in constant fear of death, the cruel enemy which had no pity, not even on a little girl like her. She had become a traumatized automaton with no will of her own, following her uncle's instructions without question. There was only one thing she did not understand.

"Uncle," she said, during one of Shmelke's rare, hurried visits, "What have I done wrong? Why do I have to hide? Am I a bad girl?"

Shmelke hugged the little girl, tears pouring down his thin, careworn face. "Matti, you're not a bad girl. You're a very good girl. But you are a Jew, like me and all the other Jews, and the Germans want to kill all the Jews, even the little children. I don't want them to get you. That's why you have to hide."

One night she was caught. A neighbor had seen her, and like a good citizen, he hurried to the police to inform on her and receive his pitiful kilogram of sugar in reward. She was sent to Pionki, where the inmates of the ghetto had been deported earlier. Much to her surprise, she found Shmelke there too. The protection provided by his papers had run out.

Pionki was a labor camp, and Matti was put to work making gunpowder. She and her work partner, another youngster like herself, could barely lift the 100 kg. bags of finished powder they were expected to stack in neat piles. They literally felt their weakened bodies breaking under the load. Lack of food and sleep aggravated the nightmarish situation. However, this period soon came to an end.

The word spread like wildfire through Pionki: all the laborers were being transferred to an extermination camp. Out of nowhere, Matti's Uncle Shmelke came running towards her. He grabbed her hand and whispered urgently, "Matti, follow me. Don't make a sound." He led her to a pit in the ground and said, "This is our bunker. We'll hide here until the Germans are finished with their devilish work. We're going to live to tell the world what happened here."

At night, Shmelke made a tiny breach in the bunker's camouflaged cover to allow some fresh air into the dank pit. The crack, miniscule though it was, was enough to give them away to two camp guards patrolling the grounds in search of fugitives such as they.

"Now would you look at that," they said gleefully, "What have we here?" The malicious joy in their voices chilled the blood in the veins of the cornered Jews.

"So much for your dirty Jewish tricks," one said glowingly, rubbing his hands together in anticipation of the kill. "Haven't you vermin learned yet that you can't fool us?"

"Enough talk!" interrupted his companion, "I'm going to kill them right now!"

"No," said the first one stubbornly, "I'll kill them. I was the one to find their rotten bunker."

"Quiet! I am your superior and I will kill them!"

There was no doubt in the Germans' minds that the two trapped Jews were going to be shot; their only question was who would have the pleasure of doing it.

Matti was indifferent. What did it matter which of them shot her, as long as they did it quickly and got it over with? She had no strength left to struggle, but Shmelke was not ready to give up. His mind raced with possible plans for their escape. When the opportunity presented itself, he seized it immediately.

As it happened, their captors were in a playful mood. Since they could not decide who would do the shooting, they ordered Shmelke and Matti out of the pit while they conferred. A third young guard joined them and suggested, "Why not have a trial? We'll court martial them, and then we can kill them."

The original pair were unsure of how to react to this idea. Shmelke took advantage of their uncertainty and whispered to his terrified, trembling niece, "Matti, run! Follow me!"

Shmelke broke into a crazed, zigzag run, darting first right, then left, with Matti hard on his trail. Even when they heard the shots behind them, they did not slow down. The bullets whistled past their ears, and Matti began to cry in terror. "Uncle Shmelke, I just can't go on any more! You keep going, and leave me here," she pleaded.

But Shmelke refused to weaken. "Just a little more, my Matti, just a little more," he insisted.

They kept running, with the Germans in hot pursuit. The bullets whizzed past them, but missed their mark. Suddenly Shmelke saw some woods up ahead. He ran towards them, pulling Matti along after him.

Abruptly, the shooting stopped. Shmelke allowed himself a sigh of relief. This is it, he thought, we're saved. The two of them collapsed on the wet earth, too exhausted to move. Their bones ached and their breath came in harsh, rasping gasps. They had not fully recovered from their ordeal when they heard the sound of a fast approaching motorcycle. Before they knew what was happening, its rider, a German major, had his gun pointed in their direction.

"*Jude!*" he roared, "Don't move!"

Shmelke and Matti tried to stand on their shaking legs. They heard the labored breathing of the German soldier as he ran towards them. He was followed by the soldiers who had found their hideout in the camp.

"*Herr Major*," said one, with a smart salute, "These Jews were discovered hiding in a bunker to avoid transfer. Furthermore, they took advantage of some momentary indecision about how to kill them and escaped. Surely the Herr Major will agree that they deserve to die on the spot."

The major looked at the grimy young soldier, still breathless from the exertion of the chase. Rather than simply pull the trigger and end the discussion, he surprised them all by saying, "Not so fast. We are not barbarians. We are civilized people. These miserable Jude are going to be tried in court." There it was again - a trial.

There was no choice but to obey.

For many long, nerve racking hours, Matti and her uncle hovered between life and death. Shmelke helped Matti say as much of *Viduy*, a Jew's final confession, as he could remember. He tried to raise the little girl's spirits, and his own as well, as best as he could. At last the court was ready to announce the verdict.

"The two prisoners, the man and the child, will be temporarily relocated to a nearby labor camp where there is a shortage of workers," was the surprising decision. It seemed that Shmelke and Matti had been granted yet another reprieve.

Matti never saw her beloved uncle again. She was assigned to the camp kitchen. The cooks, prisoners themselves, pitied the small, frail young girl, and did their best to lighten her workload. They all knew that their stay in this camp was a temporary one; their final destination would be the gas chambers. Matti wasn't there for long. She was transferred to Ravensbruck, where the women and girls, Matti among them, were forced into backbreaking hard labor from daybreak to midnight. Yet somehow, they still hoped for better days ahead. While the others dreamed of returning to their homes and children, Matti dreamed of going back to school.

Matti's dreams faded when they were all sent to the infamous punishment block. This cell, where inmates were punished for violations of the inhuman camp laws, was notorious even in the gehenna of Ravensbruck. In the punishment block, limbs were torn from the live bodies of the prisoners. They were tortured until they had no strength to stand, then shot through the head. The bodies were stacked and sorted: gold teeth, hair and even skin were removed and used by the Germans. Now Matti and her barrack mates were there, waiting.

Finally, one night they were ordered outside into the freezing cold, with only a thin piece of cloth for protection. They shivered as they waited, wondering why they had been left alone until now, and what grisly form of death awaited them. It was odd - even with death around the corner, the younger girls clustered together to play school. They recited poems they knew by heart and told each other stories of their own school days, in a world that was gone forever. The older women wept at their innocence. How could they have known that the girls' dream was about to come true?

They waited outside until sunrise. Then the Germans grabbed them and ripped the numbers off their tattered clothing. They were pushed into buses, which, they later learned, were sent by the Red Cross. They could not believe the reassuring words of the polite women who welcomed them aboard. Even as they wolfed down the generous food parcels distributed on the buses, they planned their escape. Many of them would never find out that escape was no longer necessary; they died almost at the very moment of their liberation. Their starved systems could not tolerate the huge quantities of food that they had hungrily and hurriedly ingested.

Matti was alive. Together with the surviving members of the group, she was brought to Denmark. Despite the warm and compassionate welcome they received from the Danes, Matti still could not believe that her suffering had come to an end. Then she met Rav Binyamin Zeev Jacobson. His warm smile and long beard reminded her of home, and Matti knew at once that she could trust him. She had no doubts about whether or not to accept his offer to join the new school in Lidingo.

Matti, with her hair-raising history, was one of the first ten girls to come to Lidingo. The very first question she asked the Rebbetzin on her arrival was, "When do we start school?"

"Tomorrow morning, G-d willing," the Rebbetzin assured her, amazed at the girl's fierce desire to learn.

But the next morning was a disappointment, and not only for Matti. This was a school? Without a blackboard? Without desks and chairs? Without books? The girls were disgruntled. They felt that they had been deceived. They had been told that they were going to a school, and this shabby old place didn't look like a school at all! But the Rebbetzin, serenely brought the girls to order and started teaching, the first of many enlightening lessons to come. The missing blackboard, desks, and chairs were forgotten as the girls hung on the Rebbetzin's every word. Her excitement over *Rashi's* commentary on *Chumash* was contagious - the girls knew they had come to the right place after all.

Inauspicious beginnings notwithstanding, Lidingo soon became a proper school in every respect. The Swedish government provided all the necessary supplies and fixtures, and new girls and additional teachers began to arrive. Those of the girls who had been serious students before the war, like Matti, picked up right where they had left off.

* * *

Matti's desire to learn was unabated. True, tomorrow, she would have to be punished, and she would not participate in the Rebbetzin's class. But then, she told Nechama with a mischievous grin, hadn't the Rebbetzin told them about Hillel the Elder, who had listened to a lecture from the roof of the Study Hall when he was denied admission? She could always learn a lesson from Hillel, and listen from the hallway...

"Matti, you're impossible!" laughed Nechama.

"You may be right," Matti laughed back.

Comforted, the two girls went to sleep at last, looking forward to another new day at Lidingo.

Kaddish

The girls in Lidingo knew that their relatives - parents, grandparents, brothers, sisters, uncles, aunts, and cousins - had perished in the Holocaust. Some had witnessed their deaths with their own eyes, while others heard the tragic news from other survivors. Some of the girls had no one left at all, and Lidingo was their whole world. Yet the subject was never openly discussed, and deep in their hearts, many of them still cherished the hope that someone, somewhere, was still alive, just waiting to be discovered. Perhaps it was this secret hope that made a certain announcement by Rav Jacobson so devastating.

It was the day before the fast of the Tenth of *Teves*. The girls learned in class about the destruction of the Temple, and the siege of Jerusalem which had been the beginning of the end. It was easy for them to identify with what they learned; the destruction they had recently experienced would be engraved on their hearts and in their minds forever. They also learned about the reasons that had caused the destruction. The girls resolved to strengthen their faith and do their part to prevent the recurrence of the disaster: "A generation in whose time the Temple is not rebuilt, is as if it was destroyed in its time."

The sun set early on the short winter afternoons. The girls assembled in the Green Hall for afternoon prayers. When they were done, Rav Jacobson entered the room with an unusually serious expression on his face. He asked for the girls' attention. "Tomorrow is the Tenth of

Teves. The *rabbanim* have chosen this date as a `Universal Day of *Kaddish'* for the victims of the Holocaust. Those of you who do not know the exact date of their relatives' deaths should keep this day as their *yahrzeit.* I will say *Kaddish* for them myself."

The reaction was immediate and overwhelming. The girls burst into bitter, heartrending tears. No one heard the rest of the Rav's words. As their eyes wept for their loved ones, their thoughts strayed far away, to other times and places. During those painful moments, their ears rang with bloodcurdling cries. As if it was yesterday, they could hear their little brothers' pleas that the murderers leave Mamma alone, and the shots which killed them. They relived the days when the Germans barked at them without letup as they marched, marched, marched, without food to keep their tired souls in their broken bodies. Then would come the crack of the rifle, the thud of the fallen bodies, and the last whispered words of prayer. They shivered at the memory of the anguished cries of those burned alive in the death camps. The dreadful quiet which always followed the last *Shma* was almost worst than the noise...

Suddenly the girls faced the irrefutable fact that their dear ones were really gone, never to return. Rav Jacobson's announcement was a confirmation of this agonizing realization, never articulated and never fully believed. In that one moment the illusions were smashed, to be replaced by anguished acceptance of the bitter truth.

Rav Jacobson understood what his words had meant to the girls. He allowed them a few moments to think and cry before he began to speak in a quiet, subdued voice. "My children, I can guess the thoughts going through your minds right now. I know that you are remembering your fathers and mothers, your brothers and sisters, your homes. But there is something I want you all to know."

He cleared his throat and raised his voice. The girls' controlled themselves and listened.

"Crying is good for us. Sadness in the face of tragedy is permitted. But depression is forbidden! Depression borders on despair, and a Jew never despairs of G-d's mercy. We are permitted to grieve, but we must remember that grief is not enough. We have to honor the memory of our parents and all the holy souls who gave their lives to sanctify G-d's Name by sanctifying our lives. By observing G-d's laws, by establishing observant Jewish families, we will show the oppressor *Amalek* that the Jewish people can never be destroyed: the nation of Israel lives forever. This is our goal here in Lidingo - to live in keeping with G-d's Torah, so that our lives will be worth living."

The atmosphere of depression that filled the room eased as the girls listened to the Rav's wise, comforting words. They would never forgot their families, but they could still live meaningful lives. Even if their parents were gone, they could honor and preserve their memories for the generations to come.

"Who by Water, Who by Fire"

Ahuva, one of the first teachers at Lidingo, was the descendent of a distinguished rabbinical family from Slobodka, Lithuania, and a concentration camp survivor. Her knowledge of Hebrew was excellent, and she proved a valuable addition to the religious studies staff. Although her personality was very different from her fellow teacher Chaya's, they worked together harmoniously for the well-being of the girls. Actually, Ahuva had met Chaya during the war, but they had not really gotten to know each other, and certainly had no idea then that one day they would be teaching together in a religious girls' school in Sweden.

* * *

Ahuva was in Stutthof, where women and girls suffering from typhus ended their lives in the gas chambers. By some miracle, Ahuva did not contract the disease during her entire stay in the camp.

Conditions in the camp deteriorated from day to day as more and more women, and eventually the camp guards themselves, fell victim to the dreaded disease. The prisoners received no medical attention whatsoever, nor was any effort made to alleviate their suffering. They lay on their wooden bunks, crying out for food and water. Ahuva, was assigned to serve as their nurse along with several other Jewish women.

In the meantime, the Allies were pushing forward in the war against the Axis, and had taken a considerable amount of territory. In their strongholds all over Nazi occupied Europe, the Germans were suddenly uneasy. Yet even while the prospect of defeat stared them in the face, the crematoria worked overtime. When the Germans realized that their time was running out and their crimes would soon be exposed by the advancing Allied troops, they instituted the infamous death marches. For days and nights on end, the remaining Jewish prisoners, the last tottering survivors of the camps, were forced to march endlessly forward, without food, water, or a moment's rest. Many could not endure this final torture and died of exhaustion as they marched. Those who could not keep up were shot, and their bodies left unburied on the roadside.

Stutthof was no exception. The camp commandants knew the end was near, and that all too soon, their prisoners would turn witness against them. This was something to be avoided at all costs: the prisoners would have to be eliminated.

The decision to kill all the Jews in Stutthof was not a difficult one for the Germans. The question was how to do it. They wanted to stage what would look like an accidental death, so that no one would accuse these arch-murderers of actually killing thousands of innocent people. They hit upon a novel idea. They would drown them.

Thousands of sick women and girls were jammed onto the decks and hold of a small freighter, flying a quarantine flag to keep away the curious. Not a crumb of bread or a drop of water was brought on board for the patients, who were so tightly packed together that movement was impossible. The flag was enough to keep any other ships far away. It wasn't hard for the unfortunate women to guess the purpose of the trip. As soon as the boat put out to sea, the Germans got to work. As casually as if they were playing ball, they began to shove girls and women overboard. It wasn't even a struggle - resistance was futile. Most of the women were too sick and weak to attempt to stay afloat. Those who did try to keep their heads above water were shot, leaving a pool of blood on the water as their only monument. The women on deck were in the worst condition, and they were the first to go. When they were done there, the German 'heroes' went down to the hold and selected the next batch of victims. "Now you, and you, and you," they would point. The walking skeletons had no choice but to follow them up and share the fate of their companions.

Chaya was in the hold, together with her adopted sister Dinush Melamed and Ahuva, the only healthy woman on the entire ship. They had never really met before, but Chaya knew who Ahuva was because of her unusual position in the camp. A German walked in on them and surveyed the crowded, filthy, stinking mass of humanity. Obviously, he decided, this was a place that needed to be cleared out as quickly as possible. He started pointing: "You, and you, and you." Suddenly, he turned to Ahuva and added, "And you."

"Me?" said Ahuva innocently, "Why me?" Her physical strength had failed long ago, but her mind was still clear. "You must be making a mistake. I'm not a typhus patient. I'm healthy!" She tried to smile as proof that she was indeed well.

Now he recognized her - she was the one who had cared for the patients in Stutthof. Inexplicably, he changed his mind. "Alright," he said, "Not you. At least not now."

It was nothing short of a miracle.

Chaya too was granted a miracle. A German soldier grabbed her with the cynical comment, "Now you're going to the fish." He looked at her face, which was covered with typhus sores.

"Why bother throwing me over?" asked Chaya boldly, "Can't you see I'm going to die soon anyway?"

For some reason she never understood, he left her alone.

For the moment, Chaya's and Ahuva's lives had been spared, but that was not the end of the story. The ship and its woebegone passengers were still out at sea when they heard the unmistakable sound of aerial bombardment. The prisoners down in the hold had no way of knowing what was happening. There was a terrible commotion in the stern. Then the ship took a direct hit from an American shell. Half the freighter burst into flames and sank immediately, taking with it many of the prisoners and most of the German crew.

Ironically, the same shell which sealed their fate saved the lives of the approximately two hundred girls and women in the half of the ship still precariously afloat. They were alive, but they had been wounded by shrapnel and were stranded at sea. Their cries reached the very heavens, but who would rescue them? Tongues of flame licked at the lonely ship, which began to dip alarmingly low under the weight of its cargo. The engines were there, but there was no one to man them. The few remaining Germans hurriedly took to the lifeboats, but it was too late. The rubber boats were riddled with holes and as the women watched, they went under with their frantic passengers. Those who still could crawled up to the deck, had the full horror of the scene unfolded before their eyes. It was not a sight any of them would ever forget.

Ahuva, Chaya, and Dinush were among the survivors, but there was not much cause for celebration. Literally trapped between the devil and the deep blue sea, it seemed that they were going to die now, just as they were freed from their German captors. They knew that their only help could come from G-d. Desperate and hopeless as the situation seemed, they could still pray, and so they did.

Inevitably, the ship began to come apart. Wooden beams fell away until all that was left was something resembling a gigantic raft. The women grabbed at the pieces of wood for support, fearful of toppling overboard and drowning. Night fell, but the survivors dared not close their eyes. Through it all, they trusted in G-d's mercy and did not despair. Some thought they could see the coast in the distance, but no one knew if it was real, or a figment of their urgent, wishful thinking. Propelled by the wind and the waves, they floated over the peaceful waters. There was no sign left of the nightmare they had witnessed just a short time earlier.

And then it happened: the miracle materialized. A ship was approaching! Without stopping to consider that it might be a German one, they waved vigorously, trying to attract its attention. The ship drew nearer. The sailors threw down lines and pulled the women aboard. To their horror, it soon became apparent that it really was a German ship, whose officers had seen the flames and come, too late, to their sister ship's aid. Realistically, they had not expected to find any survivors - certainly not Jews.

The prisoners were at the end of their tether. They lay on the deck unable to move. After a short discussion, the Germans decided that at this stage, it was in their own best interests to help the pathetic group of Jewish women. It was April 30th, 1945, and Hitler, may his memory be blotted out, had committed suicide that very day. The Third Reich was finished, and it behooved these members of the Master Race to provide themselves with character witnesses. They gave the women water and rudimentary care, in the hope that they would later testify on their behalf.

They were coming closer and closer to shore. Thankfully, they landed at Allied occupied Kiel, and thus were greeted by Allied soldiers, who immediately undertook to care for the survivors. (Among them was Dinush Melamed, who was extremely ill. She was separated from Chaya, and they did not meet again until the surprising encounter in a Swedish hospital.) From Kiel the group eventually went on to Sweden, where the luckier ones found Lidingo.

Ahuva too reached Sweden. After some time in a quarantine camp, she went to one of the recuperation centers established for the refugees by the kindhearted Swedes. They were treated well and received devoted care from Swedish medical personnel, who could not conceal their shock at their dreadful condition.

Much to Ahuva's surprise, one day she got a letter. She was terribly excited; she had forgotten what a letter looked like. In those days, Ahuva saw herself as someone who no longer existed as a person, and was totally worthless. Then, all of a sudden, there was a letter with her name on it: this must mean that to someone, somewhere, she still was a human being! Ahuva carefully opened the envelope, prolonging the lovely moments of delicious anticipation. It was from the *Vaad HaHatzalah*: was there anything they could do to help?

The letter could not have come at a better time. Rosh Hashanah was fast approaching, and Ahuva had been troubled by the question of where she would spend the holidays. Kind as her Swedish benefactors were, her spiritual thirst could not be quenched by the care provided in the center. Here was the perfect solution! She wrote back to the *Vaad* at once, asking to be placed with a religious family for the holidays, so that she could pray as she had in her parents' home.

At that time, the refugees in Sweden were not permitted to visit the major cities without a sponsor. A Swedish family obligingly invited Ahuva and a friend to Stockholm. The friend chose not to make the trip, and Chaya went in her stead. Ahuva and Chaya stayed with the Jacobsons, who told them all about Lidingo and took them to see it. To their delight, after the holidays they were offered teaching positions there, which they eagerly accepted. So it came about that these two wonderful young women began their holy work as teachers in Lidingo, where they gave, and received, love and devotion without measure.

The Wedding

What follows was a typical conversation among the girls in Lidingo; the names of the girls participating changed, but the content remained much the same.

"I'm never going to get married. Not ever."

"Neither will I."

"Me neither."

"It's strange, but I really used to think that when I grew up I would get married. I even tried to picture what my future husband would look like."

"But now we're grown up... Now we understand..."

"You're right. We're all going to stay together in Lidingo forever. This is our home!"

"I think that I will get married someday," interrupted Malinka. "Whenever G-d decides to send me someone suitable."

"Get married? Are you crazy?"

"Why not?" countered Malinka.

"What do you mean, why not? Are you blind, Malinka? Don't you see what's going on around you? Look at the Swedes, the people who are so good to us. They just walk around and go shopping as if nothing happened, as if people haven't been burned alive..."

"They're not normal!"

"Why aren't they normal?" Malinka persisted, "Sweden wasn't affected by the war. They only know what they saw, and for them, life goes on."

"That's just it! That's why they're not normal. Don't you understand? We, who saw it all, know things they'll never know. They'll never understand. They're different - abnormal!"

"Also the Jews?"

"First of all, how many Jews survived? Besides, the people who weren't there, even if they're Jews, don't know or understand either. We're the ones who were tested, and with G-d's help, we withstood the test. We learned to be strong and we survived. But them? What do they know? Who are they, and who are we? Could you marry a person like that?"

Malinka did not answer. Instead, she considered her friends' words. This was not the first time the girls had discussed this. The girls were growing up, and some of them were already young women. But they could not accept the fact that for most of the world, life went on, as if nothing had happened. They sensed that those who had been spared the agonies of the Nazi inferno would never understand them. There was simply no comparison between the lives of those who had been there, and those who had not. All they wanted was to remain in Lidingo forever, to study and broaden their knowledge of Judaism, and to improve their level of faith and Torah observance.

Fortunately, however, with time, they began to change their minds. The soothing, therapeutic atmosphere of Lidingo and their own success in adapting to new, normal, lives healed the girls' tortured souls, and eventually, they were able to look forward to building homes of their own.

During the years in Lidingo, most of the girls were too young to marry. As for the older ones, it was impossible to find suitable matches for them in the assimilated Swedish Jewish community. Consequently, most of the girls married in *Eretz Yisrael*, where Rav and Rebbetzin Jacobson helped them find their destined life partners. Some of the girls had left Lidingo earlier, to join relatives in the United States. Within a short time, the joyous news of their engagements and subsequent marriages began to arrive in Lidingo. One of these girls was Raizy, whose story appears in the beginning of this book.

Faigie's story was exceptional, even for Lidingo. She came to Lidingo from the camp in Faernabruk, and adjusted easily to the religious studies and spirit in Lidingo. One day a young man came to the school and asked to see her. He explained to the Rebbetzin that he was a cousin of Faigie's who had survived the war. Not long afterwards, they were married in Lidingo.

Words cannot describe the excitement of all the girls prior to and during Faigie's wedding. They had done a magnificent job preparing: they had baked and cooked, arranged the flowers, and set the tables. Dozens of loving hands turned Lidingo's dining room, an unassuming hut, into a glittering banquet hall for one wonderful day. Even the sun participated in the festivities, smiling down benignly on the new couple from on high. It seemed that the entire world beamed as Faigie, the bride, dressed in a dazzling white gown, marched over the fresh grass to join her husband to be under the wedding canopy.

First wedding in Lidingo

The groom addressed a moving plea to the Creator to complete the work of creation, and allow their marriage be a triumphant answer to the Nazi *Amalek* who sought to annihilate the Jewish nation.

The week of *sheva brachos* following the wedding was also celebrated in Lidingo. Faigie and her husband had hoped to emigrate to *Eretz Yisrael*, but were unable to obtain the necessary certificates. Instead, they settled for a new beginning in the United States. All the Lidingo girls saw them off at the bus station, showering them with loving good wishes, flowers, and gifts. For perhaps the first time in its history, the streets of the quiet town resounded with the words of *Od Yishama*, the traditional wedding song expressing the Jewish people's hope for the imminent redemption of our scattered nation: "There will yet be heard in the cities of Judea and the streets of Jerusalem the voice of joy and the voice of gladness, the voice of the bridegroom and the voice of the bride."

Amen!

A Living Casualty

Yocheved heard whispering and turned her head. It was Devora.

"Oh, it's you, Devora," she said pleasantly, "Hi."

"Shh, not so loud," whispered Devora furtively, "Be quiet and come with me. Don't you remember I told you I'd show you a secret?"

"Alright," said Yocheved in an obliging whisper.

"No, wait," said Devora suddenly, "First you have to give the password."

"Password? What password?"

Devora looked at her reprovingly. "The password of the underground, of course."

"The underground!?"

"That's right, the underground. I have my own underground, and I'm the commander!" To Yocheved's astonishment, Devora straightened her back and saluted smartly. Yocheved smiled uneasily.

"Insubordination!" snapped Devora angrily, "That'll get you three days solitary confinement! Follow me." She pointed to the right, urging Yocheved along.

This was too much. "Devora, what on earth is going on?"

"What's going on?" Devora repeated. "It's very simple. I told you I'm the commander and you didn't salute. And now you also questioned orders. For that you get another two days in solitary."

Yocheved didn't know whether to laugh or cry. She followed Devora behind the house to an open area under a big tree, which the girls called 'the square'.

"Pe, fam, fo," said Devora, and burst out laughing. She laughed and laughed until Yocheved found herself laughing as well. Perhaps it had all been a joke...

Devora was Yocheved's roommate. She had arrived in Lidingo after Yocheved, and Yocheved and her friends did everything they could to help her adjust and get settled. Devora proved to be a very likable and friendly girl, who spoke freely with everyone and told all kinds of stories about herself and her past. Some of her stories were rather odd, but the girls were understanding and everyone treated her kindly.

One night, Sara woke up and couldn't fall back asleep. She had a pounding headache, so she stepped out into the corridor, hoping the fresh air from the big hall window would help her feel better. She was greeted by a low humming sound. To Sara's surprise, she found Devora out in the hallway, wearing her new robe, softly humming an unfamiliar tune and - dancing. Her hands were outstretched, as if extended to the other dancers in a non-existent circle.

Devora glanced at her briefly. "Shh... shh," she whispered, continuing her eerie dance. Sara, headache forgotten, stood and watched, mesmerized. Devora danced beautifully, with total concentration. From time to time she would switch tunes to match the style and tempo of the dance. During these interludes, Sara tried to speak to her, but Devora merely shook her head and said, "Shh... shh..."

Sara looked out the window. The moon was the only other witness to Devora's strange behavior; it occurred to Sara that it probably understood Devora better than she did! In the dark, silent corridor, Devora's persistent humming was beginning to annoy Sara. However, she was accustomed, as they all were, to Devora's idiosyncrasies, and kept quiet. Then she heard Devora whisper something.

"Tram faglah min sharbat."

"What?" said Sara, "I don't understand."

"I said, don't tell anyone."

"Oh. What language were you speaking?" The girls in Lidingo spoke a number of languages, depending on their country of origin, and Sara assumed that Devora was speaking in her native tongue.

"It's my language," said Devora proudly, "I invented it." Before Sara could frame a suitable reply, Devora added, "What do you think of the dances? Aren't they maglud?"

"Maglud?" asked Sara weakly.

"Charming. In my language."

"Oh, sure, Devora, they were very nice. But why in the middle of the night?"

Devora turned serious. "Look," she explained, "If you want something to happen at night, you have to prepare for it at night."

Sara was tired. She was sorry she had gotten up, and all she wanted was to get back to bed.

"Goodnight, Devora," she said, heading down the hall. But Devora grabbed her arm and held her back.

"Don't think I was just dancing for the fun of it. I was practicing."

"For what?" asked Sara rather impatiently.

"For the wedding."

"Whose wedding?"

"Mine!" announced Devora happily.

"Yours!?"

Devora decided to tell her secret. "That's right. I'm getting married tomorrow night."

"Ohhhh. I mean, uh, sure you are, Devora." Sara's voice trembled as comprehension slowly dawned. "Uh, well then, *mazal tov*, Devora."

"The same to you," answered Devora gaily, "But I think you're right. We'd better get back to sleep. We need to save our strength for the wedding."

For Sara, the night was over. She couldn't get Devora's strange behavior out of her mind. This wasn't the first time she had wondered about her roommate's behavior, but she had always accepted it as a joke; they all did. Now, however, it looked like things were more serious than anyone realized. She made up her mind to speak to the Rebbetzin about what had happened first thing in the morning.

The Rebbetzin listened carefully to every word of Sara's recital. "How long has this been going on?" she asked.

"I think since she came to Lidingo," said Sara.

"Sara, you did the right thing by coming to me now. I know it wasn't easy for you. I also know you only did it for Devora's good, so don't worry about it being *lashon hara*. It's not."

That afternoon, the Rebbetzin told Mrs. Igell what she had heard. "Do you think you can find the time to speak to Devora and see what's bothering her?" she asked.

"Of course," said Mrs. Igell, "G-d willing, the very first chance I get."

Mrs. Igell's opportunity was not long in coming. During the next day's recess, she found Devora sitting by herself on the lawn, energetically uprooting leaves and grass. She sat down next to her and said, "Hello, Devora."

"Hello," replied Devora, without lifting her head.

"Is something wrong, Devora? Do you want to tell me what's on your mind?"

Devora welcomed the invitation; she loved to speak about herself. The two went for a walk, and Devora launched into a long, complicated tale, with herself as the heroine.

Listening to Devora talk, it didn't take Mrs. Igell long to grasp the problem. Devora was incapable of distinguishing between fact and fantasy. Most of her stories were beautiful wishes, which in Devora's imagination had already come true. As they neared the end of their walk, Devora suddenly blurted out, "It really hurt alot. When they beat me, I mean. On my head, here. They always hit me on the head with a club, the Nazis and the *kapo*."

Mrs. Igell stopped short; Devora's words had reminded her of an almost forgotten incident.

A group of women had come to Lidingo before the holidays, not realizing that Lidingo was a girls' home. But no one had wanted to send them away, so rooms were found for them until after the holidays. One of them, a woman of about forty, was given a job in the kitchen.

Devora was still relatively new in Lidingo, but she had already made friends with everyone and been assigned the usual chores they all shared. Shortly after the arrival of the women's group, Devora was on kitchen duty for lunch. Along with the others, she helped set the tables and began to serve the food. She lifted a pot of boiling soup and carried it to one of the tables. Suddenly she let the pot drop and it fell to the floor with a resounding bang, splashing in all directions. The girls jumped back in alarm. Devora was as white as a sheet and speechless. She stood facing the new cook, and her stony gaze wandered off to another time and place... Then she burst out screaming.

"It's you! You! I wish you were dead! When are they going to do to you what you did to us, you Nazi?" she cried hysterically. "Don't move! Stay right where you are! I'm going to get a club and give you a taste of your own medicine, straight across the head like you gave me."

Devora turned, ready to go in search of a club, but the Rebbetzin stopped her. At first the girls thought she was going to push the Rebbetzin away, but she did not. Instead, she collapsed into her arms, crying uncontrollably. The Rebbetzin let her cry, feeling her pain, as her blouse grew wetter and wetter with Devora's tears.

The cook remained riveted in place. Devora pointed an accusing finger at her and hissed, "It's her. She was the *kapo* in our last barracks. The beast was worse than the Germans!"

All the horrors of the recent past were mirrored in her round, hate-filled eyes. "If any of us managed to hide a piece of bread or a potato peel, she always knew. She would grab the girl, steal her miserable treasure, and beat the daylights out of her. She was even capable of handing her over to the Germans, and then it was all over... They either beat her to death, or shot her, or - well, they had plenty of ways to do it. And she," said Devora, pointing at the cook, "would stand there smiling, terribly pleased with herself. Then she would warn us that this was what would happen to anyone caught stealing food. But we were so hungry we couldn't stop ourselves, even though we knew what would happen if we were caught. And she beat me too! Not just once. She did it again and again, no matter how much we cried and begged for mercy!"

Suddenly, before the Rebbetzin could understand what was happening, Devora threw herself at the cringing woman, pulled her hair, bit her hands and face, and rained blow after blow on her unprotected body. It took the combined efforts of the Rebbetzin and the girls to pull her away. The Rebbetzin led Devora out of the dining room, to a quiet spot where she could cry herself out and pull herself together.

After the holidays, the women left Lidingo. There were no further incidents, and in the bustle of daily routine, the unpleasant occurrence was all but forgotten. Life returned to normal.

This was true for the other girls in Lidingo, but not for Devora. She simply could not resume her normal pursuits. The suffering and abuse she had endured in the camps had left deep mental and emotional scars, and the shocking encounter with the *kapo* had sent her plummeting even further into her own tormented dream world.

Late one night, one of the girls thought she heard someone fumbling with the gate. Most of the girls were sound asleep, but she suffered from insomnia and was still up. Alarmed, she jumped out of bed to see who was trying to open the gate at this time of night. To her utter shock she saw Devora, fully dressed, suitcase in hand, heading for the main entrance. Was the dark playing tricks with her eyes? She ran to Devora's room to check. Sure enough, Devora's roommates were sleeping soundly, while Devora's bed was made - and empty.

She ran to Mrs. Igell's apartment. Mrs. Igell woke the Rebbetzin and the two of them went running after Devora, who was still on the grounds. Devora was startled when she saw the two women chasing her, and she started screaming.

"Don't you come near me!" she cried, "I'm going to the wedding and you can't stop me! I'm never coming back here. Don't you touch me!"

It was only with great difficulty that they succeeded in bringing her back inside. It broke their hearts, but Mrs. Igell and the Rebbetzin had to face the fact that Devora could no longer remain in Lidingo; they could not give her the help she so desperately needed. She would have to receive careful professional treatment, in a qualified facility.

The following morning, the girls assembled, as always, for morning prayers. An uncomfortable silence filled the room. Their eyes wandered, and their breathing was was loud and irregular. Suddenly they began to cry bitterly. Devora, a girl like them, who had suffered like them and wanted to live a new life, was sick, too sick even to be with them in Lidingo. She had been taken away to an institution. Their tears gave vent to their pain and sadness over this tragic turn of events. They knew all too well that if not for G-d's mercy on each and every one of them, they too could have been in Devora's place. To have seen what they had seen and retained their sanity was a manifest miracle.

Devora was alive, in good physical health with her limbs intact, but she was a casualty of the Holocaust nonetheless.

In Tomelilla

Despite what the girls thought, Sweden had also been affected, albeit indirectly, by the war. It had not participated in the fighting, but its economy had suffered and a considerable deficit had been incurred. There was a great shortage of workers, which was partially filled by a work program for the refugees who had found shelter in Sweden and received stipends from the Swedish government.

In the summer of 1946, the Lidingo girls also participated in this program. Some of them were still too sick or weak to work, and remained in Lidingo with the Rav and Rebbetzin and part of the staff. The rest were taken to a remote town called Tomelilla, from which they were sent out to the surrounding farms to harvest sugar cane.

The farmers around Tomelilla were simple people who prided themselves on their affluence. On the whole, the Swedes are extremely conservative and intolerant of change. The residents of the Tomelilla area had no interest in seeing their tranquil way of life disturbed. There had been no tourism in Sweden during the war, and strangers were an unaccustomed sight. The dramatic arrival of the Lidingo girls did nothing to allay their discomfort.

The girls' stay in the country was to last six weeks, a long enough period to call for considerable preparation. Rav Jacobson firstly sent his sons to *kasher* the kitchen which had been allocated for the girls. Then the staff arrived, armed with pots, pans, dishes, cutlery, tablecloths, towels, and more. The farmers were astounded by this strange, yet orderly, invasion. The other groups who had come to Tomelilla arrived empty-handed, content to use whatever facilities they found. Even more strange, these Jewish girls had even brought along their own cooks!

Mrs. Igell was the program's coordinator. She traveled back and forth to the scattered villages where the girls were sent to work, ensuring that their needs were met until their return to Tomelilla at the workday's end. To the farmers, the Lidingo girls were an inferior breed. They did not realize that Mrs. Igell was Jewish, even though her hair was completely covered by a turban. Ignorant of the ways of orthodox Jews, they assumed that the turban was for protection against insects and dust in the fields. Since her Swedish was excellent, they took her for one of their own and as such, a receptive audience for their anti-Semitic slurs. Mrs. Igell chose not to tell them just yet that she too was Jewish. Instead, speaking as someone they could trust, she enlightened them about Jews, the Lidingo girls in particular. She eloquently explained where the girls had come from, how they had suffered in the war, and what they were doing now.

The work program, initiated by the Swedish government for its own purposes, proved to be extremely beneficial for the Lidingo girls. For one thing, it provided them with an urgently needed break. A month and a half of vigorous physical activity in the fresh air, surrounded by the smell of moist earth, was just what they needed. The work was demanding but not exhausting, and most of them were happy to participate. Even those who were skeptical at first came to enjoy the change of routine, and found it invigorating. The work day was a long one: eight hours in the fields. But the rest of their time was their own, and they filled it with study. Rav Wolbe had joined the staff, and his daily classes in Jewish philosophy, *Chumash*, and Jewish law made a unique contribution to this special period in the history of Lidingo.

Before the girls set out for Tomelilla, the teachers had composed the following song:

Oh, Lidingo, my most precious one,
Oh, Lidingo, my most beloved one,

Although I am leaving you,
I remain with you in thought!

Oh, Tomelilla, you await me,
Oh, Tomelilla, you summon me,

I'll come at once,
But not for long,
For we must remain together.

The six weeks passed quickly, and the girls returned from the country suntanned and full of energy. But as the song said, they were happy to come home and resume their studies in Lidingo.

The following year, the proposal for another stay in the country was gladly accepted, but this time it turned out to be a total failure. The girls were sent to Toro, a village about two hours away from Stockholm. That particular summer was an exceptionally hot one, unusual for Sweden. The discomfort of the almost unbearable heat was compounded by the swarms of mosquitoes who greeted the girls no less eagerly than the local farmers. The girls quickly got into the habit of swatting at them as they worked. Chaya, efficient as always, came up with the idea of tearing a branch off a tree to use as a fan. Not only did it keep away the mosquitoes, it also created a welcome breeze. The girls may have looked like they were having fencing practice, but despite the stares of the locals, the out-sized fans did help alleviate the terrible heat that summer.

But what really guaranteed the project's failure was Matti. One day, she was stung. No one, not even Matti, knew just what had stung her, but her cries of pain nearly caused the girls to jump out of their skins. With sickening speed, Matti began to run a fever, and her knee swelled up alarmingly. Mr. Igell rushed her to a hospital in Stockholm where the doctors decided to anesthetize her, in order to drain the pus which was spreading throughout the affected area. Mr. Igell stayed with her, doing his best to cheer her and make her as comfortable as possible. When Matti woke up from the anesthesia, she found herself in a clean white hospital bed, surrounded by doctors and nurses.

"Don't worry, everything will be fine," one of the doctors assured her.

"Thank you, Doctor," she said politely, wondering at all the fuss generated by an insect bite.

"Don't be afraid. No one is going to harm you," added another.

"That's right. You're safe here. Nobody will hurt you," said a third.

Matti looked from one to another, puzzled. They looked kind and concerned, but she really had no idea what they were talking about. She felt perfectly safe, and now that her sting had been taken care of, she hadn't a care in the world. She hadn't told them she was frightened; why did they keep promising her that she was safe?

It was only later that Matti learned that under anesthesia, she had talked nonstop about hiding from the Nazis who were out to kill her, praying and pleading for help.

Matti's experience was not unusual. Other Holocaust survivors rebuilt their lives and tried to suppress their memories of the past, on the edge of the subconscious, their true feelings came out. The past could be kept at bay, but it could never be erased.

As My Parents Would Have Wanted

Gitty tapped her fingers nervously as she groped for the right words:

"Do you know what I think? If you look at what we went through, I mean, how it all happened, the way it began, I can't help but think that we were blind, or that our minds just stopped working, at least in the beginning."

The people are shipped to "labor"

Gitty's roommates looked at her curiously.

"I remember the day they put up gigantic posters in our town announcing that we were all to assemble in the square near the school at eight in the morning to get work cards. No exceptions, the posters said, and no later than 8:00 A.M. No one in our family went. My father was teaching Torah and did not want to stop, and my mother was just too busy. But alot of people did go.

"Two days later, my uncle Moishe came to our house. He told us that his wife had gone to the square and had not come back. He was heartbroken. He probably suspected he would never see her again. We didn't know it at the time, but the people who reported to the square that morning were on the first transport to Auschwitz. My uncle was left alone with my two little cousins, so he asked me to come help out."

Gitty paused. Talking about her experiences provided her with a much needed outlet, yet she feared that she might be imposing on her roommates; perhaps they were not interested in hearing more horror stories. But her friends nodded at her to continue, so she took a deep breath and went on.

"I was only thirteen then, and I dared to ask my uncle, `Why did all those people go to the square that morning? I don't understand it. Didn't they suspect anything? Why would the Nazis order tens of thousands of people to come all at the same time to register for work cards? Wouldn't it have made more sense to divide the list up alphabetically, or by neighborhood, or by age, and assign hours for everyone? And why *everyone*? Were babies and old people going to get work cards too?' I demanded. I knew he was crushed over my aunt's disappearance, but I couldn't stop myself.

"Uncle Moishe listened to me with tears in his eyes. `Gitteleh,' he said sadly, `Everything -everything - is from Heaven! G-d took away our common sense precisely in order for this to happen. He simply took it away! Look at me. Since when did your aunt go on such errands? I was always the one to take care of things like that, while she stayed home with the children and her mother. And now, of all times, she decided that she wanted to get there early, and be one of the first on line. Gitteleh,' he repeated, with a deep sigh, `It is all from Heaven.'

"Since then, I knew beyond a doubt that whatever happened to me was G-d's Will. Even if I were to become deaf and blind, it would be because this was what He wanted. Anything and everything could happen to me, to all of us. We had no control.

"I remember the day they burned our synagogue. The flames soared to the heavens, and the black smoke threatened to choke us. I remember how all the Jews in town stood and watched helplessly, crying in terrible, indescribable anguish. The community's Torah scrolls were inside, and we knew they were burning too. Then a young yeshiva student appeared. I didn't know him, but he didn't look more than eighteen years old. Without a word to anyone, he jumped into the flaming building to rescue the Torah scrolls. I watched him when he did it, and he was so sure of himself! He gave his life willingly, to sanctify G-d's Name. I think that's how it was for the religious Jews. They saw everything that happened as a heavenly decree, and gave up their lives for the sanctification of G-d's Name, like the boy in the synagogue. They didn't ask questions, because the answer was obvious."

Gitty's voice trailed off. The room was silent, and Gitty was embarrassed.

"I didn't plan to tell you all this - I don't know why I did. Maybe because we were talking about faith during the Holocaust, or maybe just because it's something I think alot about. And now, more than ever, I know and believe that everything that happened really was from G-d. Just as all His Ways are beyond our comprehension, so is what happened during the war. Those of us who remained alive have to remember, and tell others about the miracles we experienced and how we were saved."

"You know, Gitty," said Mala slowly, "You're not the only one. I also think about this alot. I think that the very fact that we were saved and had the privilege of coming here to Lidingo, where we can continue the tradition of our fathers, is also from Heaven. We could have gone along with the *Shomer Hatzair* or any of the other secular groups, and what would have happened to us then? We could easily have ended up irreligious or assimilated."

"Mala's right," said Faigie. "Look at me. I had completely forgotten what Judaism was. It's not that I wanted to, but I had been through so much. I was only nine when the war broke out, and I had to fight to survive for six years. I spent a whole year hiding in a closet. By the time the war was over and I came to Sweden, I didn't have a single relative left. I would have gone with anyone who offered me an education and a place to live. Thank G-d, as soon as I got here, Rav Jacobson came to our reception center and told us about Lidingo. He asked me if I wanted to come with him. Don't think I was so eager to get back to school - I hardly remembered what the inside of a classroom looked like. I only agreed to go with him because he reminded me of my father and grandfather and uncles. After I got here, I realized that this really was the way my parents had raised me, and the type of education they would have given me. Lidingo saved me, and gave me the chance to live the way my parents would have wanted."

Tsilinka

Big, hot tears fell from seven-year-old Tsilinka's eyes, staining her cheeks. "Don't go, Tuvia, don't go," she begged.

Tsilinka's older brother shook his head sadly. "I must, my Tsilinka, I must. You understand, don't you? I'll be back in the evening, and we'll play all kinds of games together..."

Tsilinka looked at him with tearful, understanding eyes. "I know, Tuvia, but at least promise me that you'll take care of your hands. Do you promise?"

"I'll try, my Tsilinka, I promise. Now kiss your big brother goodbye." He bent over, kissed her, and wiped away her tears. "Don't cry, Tsilinka," he said soothingly, "Everything will be all right." He hugged her tightly, and then he was gone.

"Please, G-d," Tsilinka prayed in Polish, "Protect Tuvia's fingers, so they won't be cut. Make them stay whole. Oh, Mamma," she said, turning to her mother, "I forgot. G-d doesn't understand Polish, He doesn't know what I'm saying. Mamma, teach me how to pray in Hebrew, so I can ask Him to take care of Tuvia."

Tsilinka's mother had observed the exchange between her children in silence. She too was worried about her son, who had been drafted for forced labor for the Nazis, but she ignored her daughter's words.

"Come, darling, I'll comb your hair," she said. "Which ribbons shall we put in your braids today?"

Tsilinka's mother kept talking until the little girl's tears were forgotten, along with her request.

Tsilinka's parents were not observant Jews, but nevertheless, they made an effort to keep some Jewish customs at home. At the same time, they were eager to emulate their Polish neighbors, celebrating their holidays and taking part in patriotic Polish events. They made a point of speaking only Polish at home, so that their children would be fluent in the language. The infatuation ended the day Hitler, may his memory be blotted out, invaded Poland. His Nazi troops turned on the local Jewish population with inhuman ferocity. They were not impressed with the culture and gentility of the assimilated Polish Jews; they were sent to the ghettos along with their less sophisticated brethren.

Tsilinka took the change in stride. Children are children, and they adjust to change more easily than their elders. Tsilinka paid no attention to the odd practices and strange attire of her new Jewish neighbors. Although she did not understand Yiddish, she got along very well with the other children her age in the ghetto.

By the time Tsilinka arrived in Auschwitz, she was eleven, a pitiful little *Musselman* - camp terminology for the barely breathing human skeletons who were prime candidates for the gas chambers. She was drained of all vitality and looked more dead than alive. Yet somehow, time and again, G-d protected Tsilinka, and she stayed alive. Every time she wanted to pray to G-d and ask Him to take care of her, she felt frustrated and helpless, for as she understood it, G-d did not know Polish, but she still did not know Hebrew. It was only many years later that she would learn that true prayer is received in any language by a merciful G-d, who cares for all His creatures, no matter how they address Him. Despite her language problem, however, Tsilinka still sensed that Someone was protecting her, and she was right.

* * *

Tsilinka's mother hugged her tightly, still unable to grasp that her precious little girl was really alive and at her side. Tsilinka snuggled close to her mother, basking in the warmth of her love. It had been a close call for both of them. "Tell me what happened, darling," her mother said.

Tsilinka looked younger than her eleven years, and her very presence in Auschwitz was unusual. On a day they would never forget, a selection was announced in the camp. Mengele, perhaps the most dreaded monster in the Auschwitz menagerie, had arrived in person to supervise. Thousands of women were assembled in a gigantic hall, with the murderer waiting at the entrance. With trembling hands, Tsilinka's mother had smeared some lipstick on her daughter's pale mouth and tied a kerchief on her head in an attempt to make her look older. Yet she knew Tsilinka did not have a chance, and she was at her wit's end.

Amazingly, salvation appeared in the form of the kapo from their barracks. She approached Tsilinka's mother and said, "You know the little one won't pass. Give her to me. I'll save her for you." The frantic mother was beside herself with joy, and promised the woman the world for her help. The kapo took Tsilinka's hand in her own, led her to a small room adjoining the large hall, and stood her by the door.

"Listen to me, Tsilinka. The minute you hear three knocks on this door, open it and go up the stairs right outside." Tsilinka had no idea of what was going on around her, but she heard and understood the kapo's words. She nodded her head in assent: yes, she would do as she was told.

Mengele, with his usual chilling efficiency, began the selection. The women who were still fit to work were herded onto the stairs near the door. For now, at least, they would remain alive. Their less fortunate companions were transferred to another room.

Tsilinka heard three knocks. This was it! Slowly, she opened the door. She knew she was supposed to run up the staircase nearby but she was paralyzed with fear, and her legs simply refused to obey her. She stood out like a sore thumb, and every second she spent there put her in mortal danger. But she could not move. The landings were crowded with unhappy looking women - the so-called lucky ones who were chosen to live. She looked at them pleadingly, begging them wordlessly to help her escape. Their eyes filled with tears, but they had to look away. If any of them made a move to save Tsilinka, she would forfeit not only her own life, but quite possibly the lives of the entire group. Her mother was in that group, but she was too far away to reach Tsilinka in time.

Suddenly, Tsilinka felt herself being lifted by strong arms. A man embraced her and stared at her face. Trembling, Tsilinka forced herself to raise her eyes and look at him. Her breath caught in her throat and her heart literally stopped beating. She was in Mengele's arms!

For a moment he tightened his grip. "That's it, little girl," he said, deathly calm, "The game is over. Now you're going to die!" He carried her emaciated body to the room where some sixty women awaited the end. As casually as if she was a sack of flour, he threw her to the floor.

Tsilinka dragged herself upright with great difficulty. Every bone in her body ached from the fall. Her eyes searched for her mother in the crowded room, if only to say goodbye. Her mother had promised her they would die together, in each other's arms. As Tsilinka looked around the room, her desperate mother pushed her way through the crowd. Their eyes met... and Tsilinka's mother acted. She broke away from the privileged group and ran towards her daughter, determined to keep her promise. Mengele wouldn't let her.

Like the madman he was, he lashed out with his whip. "Cursed Jewess!" he screamed, "You were the one who hid her! Do you think you're going to have an easy death in the gas chambers now? You're going to die right now, while your miserable Jewish brat watches!"

Mengele whipped the defenseless woman brutally until she lay bleeding and unconscious on the floor. Tsilinka was certain she was dead. Now Tsilinka too was ready to die; she no longer had any reason to live. The kapo, whose well-intentioned attempt to save Tsilinka had ended in disaster, offered to help Tsilinka again. Tsilinka shrugged her shoulders and shook her head. What for? She remained with the women who were condemned to death.

Despite her decision, Tsilinka was afraid of death. She couldn't picture what it was like. She remembered the sickening smell of burnt flesh - human flesh - which had greeted them upon their arrival in Auschwitz, and the thick reddish smoke which wafted gracefully upward. It was the middle of night, but the Auschwitz orchestra played loudly, as ever more doomed prisoners were led on their last journey. The music was never enough to drown out the cries of the victims, and Tsilinka was to hear them repeat the same words many times, although she did not know what they meant: "*Shma Yisrael...*"

Was that what would happen to her now? Would the reddish smoke be Tsilinka's bones, ascending to Heaven? She resigned herself to death, and only wished it was over, so that she could be with her mother. A loud voice interrupted her reverie. It was a German officer.

"Everybody out. It's not worth wasting gas on just sixty Jews. You'll have to wait until tomorrow evening when a new transport arrives."

The women in the room had not spoken to each other until then. Now they exchanged horrified looks. Death was a difficult experience, but it could only happen once. Then it was over. Waiting for death was even harder: the senseless numbness, the helplessness, the memories of a life that had been too short. Now it would have to go on for another day.

Tsilinka did not talk to the women. She talked to G-d. One of the women in the camp had taught her to say a Jewish prayer, in Hebrew, as she had always wanted. It was the one she had heard the Jews say on their way to the gas chambers. She repeated it now, over and over: *Shma Yisrael, Hashem Elokeinu, Hashem Echod.* She still did not understand the meaning of the words, but she knew that G-d did, and she invested them with all the fears and emotions of an eleven year old child about to die.

The women had not eaten for two days, and they were starving. One of them plucked up enough courage to approach the bored German soldier who was guarding them. "Please," she said in a trembling voice, "We are hungry. It's two days since we've eaten. We are going to die soon anyway. What difference does it make if we at least die on a full stomach?"

To their surprise, instead of whipping the impudent woman for her insolence, the soldier nodded his head in agreement. "I need ten women," he shouted, "Two for each pot of soup!"

Tsilinka was pushed forward among the ten, and marched along with them to the kitchen. The kitchen was far removed from the crematoria. In keeping with their status as dangerous criminals, the women were escorted by a heavy guard of German soldiers and their famished dogs, who played a ghoulish role of their own in the life and death of the camp.

As they approached the kitchen, they were greeted by shouts of "Tsilinka! Tsilinka!" Tsilinka saw the familiar faces of women she knew from the camp. "Run, Tsilinka, run!" they cried.

Tsilinka looked around. Run away? What a joke! They were surrounded by soldiers and hungry dogs. Suddenly she saw her mother, beaten, bruised, and petrified. Wasn't she dead? She looked at her mother and called, "Mamma! I'm fine, Mamma! Don't worry about me, they sent us out to work. We're on our way to the kitchen for soup. They're not going to kill us."

But the women would not leave her alone. They continued to shout at her, urging her to flee. Tsilinka did not know what to do. Together with her partner, she lifted the heavy pot of soup and began the march back. It was then, just as she had given up, that the miracle occurred. The pot fell and the thin, watery soup spilled out on the ground. Like flies, the starving women descended upon it from all sides. In the ensuing confusion, Tsilinka made her escape and ran to her mother.

She told her mother everything that had happened to her, adding, "Don't you see, Mamma? That's exactly the way it was. Now I just have to learn to pray in Hebrew. G-d is watching over me, and I want to thank Him."

Tsilinka's astonishing rescue from certain death in the gas chambers reinforced her longing for prayer. She pleaded with her mother, "Mamma, teach me how to pray. I must ask G-d to watch over us, and I can't do it in Polish."

This time, her mother took her a little more seriously. "Listen to me, Tsilinka," she said, "I don't know how to pray. I also don't know Hebrew. But I promise you that if your father is still alive after the war, I will let you learn how to pray in Hebrew."

"But Mamma," protested Tsilinka, "If you don't know, then who will teach me? Will you let me go to a rabbi?"

"Alright, Tsilinka. If it means so much to you, then after the war I will find a rabbi to teach you. But remember, only if Father is still alive!"

G-d continued to watch over Tsilinka. Unable to return to their barracks, she, her companion, and her mother were slipped into a group of women whom, they thought, were boarding a train to work. Tsilinka was ridiculously out of place. These women were wearing uniforms, and they were all much older than her. But Tsilinka had no choice. Dressed only in a shirt several sizes too big for her, she joined them as they climbed into the last car of a long train, praying that no one would notice her.

After half an hour's travel, the train jolted to a halt. She almost fainted when she heard a harsh voice announce in German, "We are searching for the following numbers." The numbers were hers and that of the woman who had fled with her. And to the Germans, they were not people. They were - numbers.

Tsilinka again feared for her life. Why should these women endanger themselves for a little girl, whom they didn't even know? She turned to G-d, her Protector, whispering, "Please help me again." To her surprise, one of the women called out, "They're not in here, sir!"

The Germans, tired from searching the other cars for the fugitives, decided to believe her, and didn't bother to check Tsilinka's car.

The train was headed for the forced labor camp in Ravensbruck. The work there was not only excruciatingly difficult, it was also pointless. The women were forced to carry earth back and forth from one end of a field to the other, and to shatter rocks and collect the pieces. Tsilinka did not have the strength for it, but the kindhearted women in her labor unit helped her and covered for her constantly.

A few weeks before the end of the war, when shocking numbers of inmates at Ravensbruck were starving to death daily, a Red Cross delegation made a surprise visit to the camp, and distributed generous food parcels to each of the prisoners. The famished people devoured them instantly, and many of them paid for the parcel with their lives. Their starved systems could not tolerate the sudden increased food intake. Tsilinka and her mother, however, had eaten only small amounts of the precious food at a time, and they were unharmed. But weeks passed and the food came to an end. The prisoners' terrible hunger was matched only by their despair. Tsilinka resorted to her only solution: she prayed, asking G-d to hear and understand her pleas.

Tsilinka's prayers were answered. Count Folke Bernadotte, a Swedish nobleman, arrived at the camp to negotiate the exchange of two hundred Polish - the word Jewish was not mentioned - women for German prisoners of war. Tsilinka and her mother were among the lucky two hundred. They were brought to Sweden, to the refugee camp at Doversdorp. They were fed, examined, given medical treatment, and deloused. For the first time in years, Tsilinka found other girls her own age. She spoke with them in Polish, but noticed that they conversed among themselves in another language. She listened attentively. Could this be Hebrew?

Refugees from all over Europe had come to Doversdorp, not all of them Jewish. A number of Polish teachers opened a Christian school in the camp, which taught not only academic subjects, but religion as well, claiming that Christianity was the religion of love. Itta, a young Jewish girl, challenged this statement, blurting out, "How is it possible to massacre innocent men, women, and children, old people and babies, in the name of a `religion of love'? That's not love, it's evil! You're talking about a religion of hypocrisy!"

The confused teacher looked at her with alarmed eyes, crossed herself incessantly, and did not utter a word. What could she say? Could she honestly tell her pupils that lining up unarmed people and shooting them down in cold blood was love?

Itta remembered the ravenous dogs that had attacked the Jews in her hometown as they waited for the trains which took them to the camps. She would never forget the sight of her neighbor, a man name Yudel, who lay face down in the dirt, dead. One of the dogs had torn his throat to pieces. Itta knew she would never be able to look at a dog after that. Was she supposed to love them?

After Lidingo opened its doors, Rav Jacobson took upon himself the task of visiting the refugee camps all over Sweden, in search of Jewish girls in need of a Torah observant home. He came to Doversdorp, with a small group of Jews and what he found was a situation demanding immediate intervention.

The girls, young, confused concentration camp survivors, who had been torn away from their parents very young, and had only blurred recollections of their lives before the war. were in imminent danger of assimilating into the welcoming gentile community. Thanks to the efforts of the visiting rabbis, the Jewish girls were transferred to the camp at Helsjoen, where they would be cared for in the Jewish tradition.

Helsjoen was a model convalescent center for refugees, mostly women, who wanted to live in accordance with Jewish tradition. The conditions there were wonderful. The food was not only strictly kosher, but of excellent quality. The center itself was orderly and clean and, most important of all, an island of tranquility. The leafy trees, the fragrant wildflowers, the berries waiting to be picked, were a breath of Paradise for these people who had seen Gehenom and survived.

They went willingly. They felt like outsiders in Doversdorp, especially after Itta's outburst reminded them that they really were different from their Christian fellow refugees.

Classes in Helsjoen were run by a Jewish woman named Mrs. Dukis, a Holocaust survivor like her students. She understood the girls and taught them gradually, progressing slowly from the blessings to daily prayers before attempting more demanding material.

Most of the girls were orphans. Tsilinka was not. She urged her mother to join the Jewish group in Helsjoen, but her mother was not so sure. She had recognized the kind visitors for what they were: orthodox rabbis, a breed of which she was not particularly fond. Tsilinka, however, knew how to be stubborn, and her constant entreaties finally wore her mother down. The two of them went to Helsjoen where, the mother told herself, she would at least be on hand to keep Tsilinka from picking up any nonsense. For the first time since the Nazis invaded Poland, Tsilinka was happy; each day seemed to her to be the most beautiful of her life. After years of waiting, she had finally been granted what she had always wanted: she was learning to pray to G-d in the language He understands, Hebrew.

On the first day of class, the teacher handed each girl a flower. They thanked her and sat down. Then the teacher walked over to the window and said, "Girls, do you see how many flowers there are growing outside? There are so many beautiful ones, just like those I gave you. They're wildflowers, grown by G-d, and they are as much yours as mine, which anyone can come and pick. When I gave them to you, you thanked me. Do I deserve your thanks? No, I don't - the flowers are not mine. G-d, to whom the world and all it contains belongs, is the one we should thank for the beautiful flowers He gave us."

The girls sat quietly, intrigued. The simple words went straight to their hearts. The teacher continued.

"Think about the bread we eat. Where does it come from? From the bakery. And where does the bakery get the wheat, to make the flour to bake bread? From the farmer, of course. But how does the farmer produce the wheat? He sows grain and hopes it will grow, but he has no guarantee that it will. There has to be sufficient rainfall and good weather, so that the crops won't be destroyed. Who takes care of that? The Al-mighty."

Ten year old Laikie interrupted excitedly, "It's like baking a cake. You can prepare all the ingredients, but if you don't put it in the oven, or the oven doesn't work, or you leave it in too long and it burns, there's still no cake."

"Exactly, Laikie. Man has to do his part, but success comes from G-d. This is why we recite the Grace After Meals, to thank G-d for the food that He gives us."

On that first day, the girls learned the Grace After Meals. In a similar fashion, they learned the other blessings and the basic laws which guide a Jew in his daily life. These classes were not part of a formal school program. They were given on a volunteer basis by Mrs. Dukis, who wanted to provide at least a temporary educational framework for the children and the youth in the refugee camp. Tsilinka eagerly absorbed every word; it was all new and exciting. When she told her mother about the fascinating things she was learning, her mother looked at her quizzically but kept her silence.

Tsilinka met Rav and Rebbetzin Jacobson in Helsjoen, when they came to recruit girls for the newly opened school in Lidingo. With his inimitable smile, the Rav greeted each girl with a friendly *Shalom Aleichem*. Tsilinka had no memory of rabbis, certainly not of anyone like Rav Jacobson, who was tall and distinguished, with a long beard and expressive eyes.

But there was something which still disturbed Tsilinka terribly, although she didn't dare to admit it: the Rav spoke German. Was he a rabbi? Deep in her heart, Tsilinka was afraid that the whole thing was a German trick. One day, she feared, the Rav would change clothes, remove his beard, and reveal himself to be an SS officer in disguise, who would beat and abuse them. This fear was to haunt her even later on, when she came to Lidingo.

A number of Tsilinka's good friends were going to Lidingo, and she very much wanted to join them. But the bitter news which reached Helsjoen changed her plans. Tsilinka's father and her beloved older brother, Tuvia, were dead. Tsilinka's mother's response was one of great anguish, and equally great anger: why had this happened? Friends in the camp taught her how to observe the traditional seven day mourning period, but she refused to be consoled for her loss. She grew embittered and depressed.

Tsilinka remembered her mother's words, spoken in Auschwitz: "I promise that if Father is alive after the war, I will allow you to study with a rabbi." But her father was dead, and Tsilinka could not go to Lidingo.

She bid her lucky friends a sad farewell as they prepared to leave for Lidingo with the Rav and the Rebbetzin. When the Rebbetzin heard that Tsilinka's mother forbade her to go, she told her, "Tsilinka, this is what your mother wants. Honoring one's parents is a very important commandment in our holy Torah. You must listen to your mother."

Tsilinka sat at the camp gate until nightfall, crying tears of sorrow and envy. Almost immediately, she began a lively correspondence with her friends in Lidingo. They sang the new school's praises, describing the learning, the new friendships, the after school activities, and in general, how very happy they were to be there.

Man's salvation is a mysterious thing: one never knows when and how it will come, but the believing Jew knows that somehow, it will. At times, things we say could never happen - just do. So it was with Tsilinka and her mother, who unexpectedly received the magnificent news that Tsilinka's father was still alive!

"He's not dead, he's not dead!" trilled Tsilinka ecstatically, "Father's alive!" Her happiness was twofold. Her beloved father was alive, and now she could go to Lidingo - hadn't her mother promised?

Tsilinka's mother busied herself with inquiries as to her husband's whereabouts. Tsilinka, on the other hand, was getting ready to go to Lidingo. She wrote to her friends and asked them to find out if the Rebbetzin was willing to accept her, even though she was not (yet?) religious. At the same time, she reminded her mother of her promise. Her mother was taken aback.

"Don't you at least want to see Father, after all the suffering he's gone through?"

"Of course I do. The minute I hear from you that you've found him, I'll come immediately. But that could take a long time," she said with youthful bluntness. "What's the point of my staying around here and waiting?"

Her mother had to admit that Tsilinka was right. She had also read the exuberant letters from Lidingo, and she realized that her daughter would probably be very happy there. She gave her consent. In the meantime, Tsilinka received the Rebbetzin's reply: she would gladly accept Tsilinka in Lidingo, but only if her mother agreed.

The night before she left for Lidingo, Tsilinka was too excited to sleep. She lay awake, trying to picture the rooms and the corridors, the beautiful plants, and everything else the girls had described in their letters. How she missed them! The next day, after a very long trip, Tsilinka arrived in Lidingo, where she was given a warm welcome. The Rebbetzin came to wish her success and Mrs. Igell quickly set up a bed for her in a room with several girls her own age.

"Hey, Tsilinka!" called a familiar voice. Tsilinka was delighted to see that it was Leah, a girl she had met in Poland and who, it turned out, was actually a distant relative. Leah linked her arm in Tsilinka's. "Tsilinka," she said, "I can't believe it's really you! Tell me about everyone. How is the Perkal family? And Rochel Borkas?" She spoke in Polish, as did the other girls from Poland. Hebrew was the spoken language in Lidingo, but until the new girls were fluent, they could converse in their native tongues. Tsilinka and Leah began to tell each other all their news.

In the midst of all the excitement, a girl who was a stranger to Tsilinka passed by and blurted out, "Leah, I just wanted to remind you, don't speak any *lashon hara.*"

"What?" said Tsilinka, "*Lashon hara*? Uh, sure. I don't know how to speak *lashon hara* anyway," Tsilinka assured her, figuring that *lashon hara* must be another name for Hebrew, which she still did not understand in any case.

A few days later, Tsilinka could already laugh with her friends over the incident. She had learned that "speaking *lashon hara*" meant speaking ill of others, and that much care must be taken not to engage in such talk. Shortly after her arrival, the Rebbetzin had given an eye-opening class on the laws of lashon hara in German, which made a powerful impression on Tsilinka. For homework they were to write compositions on the subject, and Tsilinka's was so good that it was translated from Polish and displayed in the classroom. It seemed that Tsilinka was off to a wonderful start in Lidingo.

Before long, however, Mrs. Igell discovered a very serious problem. As happy and well adjusted as she appeared to be, Tsilinka was unable to eat, and the little that she did force down was vomited shortly afterwards. Tsilinka was not the only girl with this problem; a number of girls had gone on hunger strikes when they came to Lidingo. They had lost their interest in life, and had chosen this as a passive way to die. Slowly, these girls began to respond to Rav Jacobson's gentle humor, the Rebbetzin's inspired teaching, and Mrs. Igell's motherly care, and they started to eat.

But not Tsilinka. Not only didn't she eat, she also didn't sleep. For a growing adolescent who had to regain her health, this was serious business. She compensated for the lack of food by drinking milk, but she could not make up for the lost sleep, and grew paler with each passing day. She was taken to specialists in Stockholm, who were very concerned. They feared that Tsilinka's inability to eat and sleep might literally cost her her life. At first, the problem was attributed to contraction of the stomach muscles after years of hunger. But then it came to light that in Helsjoen, she had had no trouble at all sleeping and had eaten heartily. Could she just be homesick? She was sent home for a vacation, and came back in even worse condition than before. The Rebbetzin took Tsilinka to a psychologist, but he too was unable to help her.

No one knew what Tsilinka was experiencing. She couldn't bring herself to tell anyone what was really troubling her. Only years later, when Lidingo had moved to Haifa, did she summon the courage to tell the Rebbetzin the truth. The Rebbetzin was stunned to hear that Tsilinka's suffering had been caused by the girl's deep fear of... her, and of her husband, Rav Jacobson! It had begun in Helsjoen, when she heard them speaking German, and continued to torture her in Lidingo. Despite the good conditions and loving atmosphere - or perhaps because of them - she had feared that it was all too good to be true, and that one day it would all come to an end.

Every day before dawn, Rav Jacobson left his room on the top floor and went downstairs to the Igells' apartment on the first floor, to learn with Mr. Igell. Tsilinka could not fall asleep at night until she heard the Rav's cough as he went down the steps, accompanied by the ever present smell of cigar smoke. Tsilinka would shiver in her bed as she waited. Perhaps this would be the day the Rav would show his true colors. He would throw off his rabbinic garb, revealing an SS uniform, and then it would all be over... It was only when he had passed by the dormitory rooms without incident that she could relax and fall asleep for a few short hours.

Tsilinka was ashamed of her fears, and she kept them to herself. Yet as much as she admired the Rav, the Rebbetzin, and the entire staff, the only ones she felt she could really trust were Chaya and Ahuva. They too, Tsilinka knew, were Holocaust survivors, and as such, she knew they were authentic. They would never turn out to be Germans in disguise.

"Honor Your Father and Mother"

When Tsilinka's father learned that she was in a religious institution, he wrote to her, "All the rivers will eventually flow into the sea"; he understood. Her mother, however, could not accept what she viewed as a calamity. She did everything in her power to convince her to leave Lidingo. Tsilinka's visits home deteriorated into an endless round of inducement, persuasion, and enticement, but Tsilinka could not be budged. She would not give up Lidingo, which had become her second home. Regardless of her secret fears, she knew that Lidingo had given her the spiritual grounding she had so sorely missed during the difficult years of the war. Despite her initial ignorance, she fit in well, and gradually learned the basic Torah laws which were part of life in Lidingo. She was never asked to do anything against her will. Everyone accepted her as she was, and helped her in any way they could.

At first, Tsilinka found it difficult to hide her surprise at the odd behavior of her roommates. One *Shabbos* morning, she stood at the mirror in her room, combing her hair. Raizy looked at her, hesitated for a moment, and blurted out, "You can't do that on *Shabbos*, it's forbidden."

Forbidden? Tsilinka wondered. This was news to her, but if hair combing was forbidden, she wouldn't comb her hair. Eventually she asked the Rebbetzin to transfer her to another room, as she felt that her ignorance of Jewish law was disturbing to her roommates.

"Out of the question," the Rebbetzin replied. "Stay in your room with your friends. You're not a hardship for them, Tsilinka. They'll help you. Everyone learns at her own pace."

The Rebbetzin was right, of course. Tsilinka's friends were loyal and helpful. With time, she recognized the sincerity of their intentions, and began to feel more comfortable with them. The differences began to fall away, and soon Tsilinka was one of them, both in her conduct and in her fierce desire to go to *Eretz Yisrael*.

One day Tsilinka received some exciting news: her parents had obtained immigration certificates to *Eretz Yisrael!* Tsilinka was to return home immediately and prepare to leave Sweden. She was thrilled. She gleefully packed her bags and said goodbye to her envious friends, who showered her with small gifts and mementos. How they all hoped to join her soon...

As soon as Tsilinka stepped through the door of her parents' home and saw her mother's face, she knew something was wrong. It did not take long for her to learn the truth: there were no certificates, and there would be no trip to *Eretz Yisrael*. The whole thing had just been a ruse to get her home. As much as she tried to understand her parents, she felt duped and deceived, as well as angry and hurt. To her parents' consternation, she spent her time alone in her room, refusing to eat or drink. What was she supposed to do now? There were definite plans underway for all the Lidingo girls to emigrate to *Eretz Yisrael*, and now it looked like she was stuck in Europe. How proud she had been when she parted from her friends; she, Tsilinka, was to be the first to go! They probably thought she was already there, while, in actual fact, she was still at home, miserable and angry. And the worst of it was that they all would go to *Eretz Yisrael*, but without her!

Finally, Tsilinka decided to swallow her pride and write to Rav Jacobson, explaining what had happened. A few days later she received a telegram from the Rav instructing her to wait for a telephone call from him at a specific time on a specific day. What a relief! Rav Jacobson had not forgotten her. Right on time, Rav Jacobson called. To her surprise, he told her that the girls' dreams of *aliyah* had become reality, and they would be leaving the following week. Rav Jacobson had added Tsilinka's name to the list of Lidingo girls; all she needed was her parents' permission to join them. Tsilinka was ecstatic. What could be easier? Yet once again, Tsilinka had reckoned without her parents.

Tsilinka's father had recognized his daughter's anguish and decided that enough was enough. Just a few days before Rav Jacobson's call, he had registered Tsilinka for *aliyah*. The *aliyah* office had been surprised - a young girl who was lucky enough to still have parents, going alone? Hadn't she suffered enough? Tsilinka's father allowed himself to be persuaded to register himself and his wife as well. When he came home, he was able to proudly tell his daughter, "Tsilinka, dry your tears. In just one month, we are going to *Eretz Yisrael*." Tsilinka could hardly believe her ears, but she knew she could rely on her kind-hearted father, who had been so understanding of her desire to be religious.

When the Rav called, Tsilinka was in a quandary. It seemed that she really would be going to *Eretz Yisrael*, but with whom? The truth was that she would have preferred to go with her second family, the Lidingo girls, but her parents refused unequivocally. They were only going to *Eretz Yisrael* because of her. How could she leave them?

Rav Jacobson told her in no uncertain terms that she would have to be patient, and go with her parents.

"Tsilinka," he said gently, "You have done so well until now with observing the Torah's commandment to honor one's parents. Make another sacrifice now - it's really only a small one. We will meet again soon in *Eretz Yisrael,* G-d willing."

With best wishes for a safe journey and success in their new home, they parted - for the time being.

Tsilinka was one of only three Jewish children from Kielce, Poland to survive the war. Thanks to Lidingo, with G-d's help, she was not lost to her people.

I Have No Blood!

Rav Jacobson called his girls 'angels', but at the same time, they were also just human beings, as impulsive and mischievous as girls their age all over the world. It was true that the Lidingo girls worked hard on their *middos*, and a pronounced atmophere of piety pervaded the school, there were definitely girls who were only interested in study, but there were others who, quite naturally, distinctly enjoyed a bit of fun. Certainly none of them were averse to a little time off. Why not?

Not all the girls in Lidingo enjoyed good health. The effects of years of abuse and malnutrition would take some of them years to overcome. The administration took the matter of the girls' health very seriously, in light of the girls' background, they were not prepared to take any chances. Any girl who was not feeling well was expected to inform Mrs. Igell, and Mr. Igell would immediately make an appointment for a suitable doctor in Stockholm. All things considered, the girls did not mind this at all. A trip to town, even if to see a doctor, was an occasion, and they relished the opportunity to admire the shop windows on the way.

* * *

Dinush was very alarmed when she woke up one morning and found hairs on her pillow. She hurried off to Mrs. Igell and announced gravely, "I'm going bald."

"Oh?" said Mrs. Igell with a straight face, as she admired Dinush's pretty hair, "When?"

"Mrs. Igell, this is serious!" protested Dinush, "Look." She ran her fingers over her head, and sure enough, quite a few hairs came away in her hand.

"I see what you mean," said Mrs. Igell, "But don't worry - you're not going bald. You are suffering some hair loss, though. It happens sometimes, and it's easy to treat. Stop by the office on your way to class and ask Mr. Igell to make you an appointment at the hospital in Stockholm."

Dinush, still worried, hurried to the office. The story of her hair loss, and more importantly, of her impending trip to Stockholm, spread quickly, and several girls who were eager to come along approached Mrs. Igell that day, complaining that their hair was falling out too. It seemed that Dinush's doctor's visit was to become quite an outing.

A trip to Stockholm was a major event, and those participating planned their itinerary carefully. First they would go to the hospital, have their checkups, and get their medicine. That should still leave them with almost an entire day to stroll around Stockholm, window shopping and seeing the sights. They figured they'd be back in Lidingo by evening.

Much to the girls' surprise, they were greeted in the hospital by a team of doctors and interns, who gave them thorough medical examinations. Then they were told to take seats in the waiting room. They assumed that they would be handed their prescriptions and sent home, after which the day would really begin. But instead of handing out slips of paper and sending them on their way, the doctor who joined them in the waiting room made a horrifying announcement. "Girls, we're going to have to run some blood tests on you to determine why your hair is falling out," he told them.

The girls turned pale. This wasn't what they had had in mind at all!

Of all the girls in the group, Dinush, Sosha, Rocheleh, and Leah were the ones who really had a problem with their hair. But the doctor did not start with them. Instead, he turned to Sara, who had barely been able to pluck a strand of hair from her head, but had been in urgent need of a day's vacation.

"Let's start with you," he said pleasantly.

Sara didn't budge.

"Don't be afraid. It's just a little pinprick."

Sara leaped to her feet. "No, no, doctor, it's quite alright. You needn't bother," she babbled, "I don't give blood." She clutched her arm with all her might to keep it away from the doctor. "They took away all my blood in the camp, there's really nothing left. Look, you can see for yourself, I haven't any blood left to give you. Thank you, doctor, goodbye!"

Before the stunned doctor could respond, Sara vanished, along with all but four of her friends. Dinush, Sosha, Rocheleh, and Leah stayed behind, had their blood tests, and were treated. They soon recovered from their experience completely - perhaps even sooner than Sara and the others!

The New Teacher

Ahuva received her immigration certificate to *Eretz Yisrael* in the spring of 1946, and the girls greeted the news with mixed feelings. On the one hand, they envied her good luck, but, on the other, they were very sorry to see her go. In the short time she had taught in Lidingo, her pleasant personality, kind heart, and gentle manner had gained her many admirers. Now she had been traced by relatives in *Eretz Yisrael* who had sent her the longed for certificate, and she was leaving them.

The girls prepared a moving farewell party to thank Ahuva for the valuable contribution she had made to life in Lidingo and to their education. How they all hoped to join her in the Holy Land, soon!

Chaya, as always, took advantage of the occasion to dedicate a poem to her colleague, whom she had met under the worst possible conditions in Stutthof, and to whom she had become very attached in Lidingo.

You are going away, You are leaving us.
Your purpose is holy, of course,
But one thing I ask:
Don't forget your sisters,
Even when you dwell in our Land. —

We shall all go there soon
And we'll meet once again.
With G-d's help, we will do our duty,
We will add new bricks to the holy edifice,
And spread Torah among our brethren. —

We will be ready
To learn and to teach.
Goodbye to you, our sister!
May we soon meet again
In the distant land,
So close to our hearts. —

Ahuva and the girls were deeply moved. When the party ended, they all accompanied Ahuva to the bus station to see her off. Bedecked with garlands of flowers and weighed down with presents, she could hardly extricate herself from the embraces of her loving students. With tears in her eyes, she boarded the bus, leaving behind the girls whose joy for their teacher was tempered by their own sense of loss.

As soon as she arrived in *Eretz Yisrael*, Ahuva began to search for a teacher who would be willing to replace her in Lidingo. It was not easy to find someone who would be willing to part from her parents and family and leave *Eretz Yisrael* for a country as foreign as Sweden. Then she met Tzipora, a young woman, still single, whose parents had managed to leave Germany right before the outbreak of the war. Fortunately, they saw it as quite natural for their daughter to go to Lidingo, and the school gained a dedicated, talented teacher who had a great deal to offer all the girls she taught.

When Tzipora came to Lidingo that fall, she was thrust at once into a grueling schedule of almost constant teaching. Ahuva was gone, and Chaya was away in France. The Rebbetzin gave her regular classes, Mrs. Igell taught geography, and Mr. Igell, English, the rest of the curriculum was left to Tzipora, and she barely had a moment to breathe. She took her teaching duties very seriously. To her, teaching was not a job, it was a sacred task - and she acted accordingly. When Tzipora was not in the classroom or preparing lessons, she would sit and talk with the girls, who insisted that there were things she could never understand, because she had not been through the war. Despite this, they grew very fond of her. When she lost her precious pearl necklace, they spent an entire afternoon helping her search for it.

Eventually, Tzipora realized that she needed at least a little time for herself and would have to slow down. She began to take long walks in the vicinity of Lidingo and make occasional visits to Stockholm. She was profoundly affected by the magnificent view from her own window. She fell in love with Lidingo, with the bright skies and shimmering moon. She reveled in the long sunset hours and the twilight which followed them. The snowy winters, so different from *Eretz Yisrael*, reminded her of her childhood.

At times, because of the Hebrew spoken in Lidingo, Tzipora forgot that she was far from home, in distant Sweden. Several times she inadvertently referred to Lidingo as if it were in *Eretz Yisrael*. Lidingo was definitely a special entity, she knew, and she felt that she was doing the right thing in the right place.

When Chaya returned from Paris, she immediately resumed her teaching duties in Lidingo, which made life much easier for Tzipora. Chaya was warmly welcomed by the girls, who had really missed her, especially in light of Ahuva's departure. Rochke was happiest of all to see her back. While in France, Chaya had corresponded with her regularly, which meant a great deal to the girl. Chaya knew that Rochke was terribly lonely: as far as she had been able to ascertain, no one at all was left of her entire family.

There were girls in Lidingo who had never gotten mail. The staff searched for distant relatives, or surviving neighbors and acquaintances of theirs, and convinced them that an occasional letter would bring great joy to these bereft youngsters. When the other girls received mail from relatives, Rochke would stand on the sidelines, watching and wishing... For the duration of Chaya's trip to France, Rochke too had had the pleasure of receiving mail. It was personal touches such as these on the part of the teachers that made Lidingo what it was.

Dear Diary

It's been a long time since I've had a chance to write, but don't think I've forgotten you. I'll tell you what happened, and I'm sure you'll understand. But I do want you to know that I really missed you. Every night I thought of you. While all the other girls wrote in their diaries each evening, Rivka and I couldn't. Why? Be patient, and I'll explain everything.

The first thing you should know is that there are several of us who enjoy taking a trip to Stockholm every once in a while. I told you about the time when Dinush started losing her hair and we decided to take advantage of the opportunity to go along. We almost died of embarrassment when we got back to Lidingo and had to tell Mrs. Igell the truth. But we still hadn't learned our lesson, and were more than ready to try again. Then Ruthie, Rochke, and Chanke claimed they had trouble seeing the blackboard. Every time a teacher accused them of daydreaming, they would say that it wasn't their fault - they just couldn't see the board. Chaya insisted that this had to be checked out at once, and Mrs. Igell made hospital appointments for them. We certainly couldn't let a chance like this just slip by!

You guessed it. We went straight to Mrs. Igell and complained that our eyes hurt and we couldn't see well. Mrs. Igell, always kind and caring, made appointments for us as well. What more could we ask?

Anyway, the big day came and there we were, at the hospital in Stockholm. We went straight up to the ophthalmology department, where each of us was examined by an eye doctor. I don't know what happened to the others, but I'll tell you what happened to me. Now, the truth is that, thank G-d, my eyesight is excellent and I've never had any pain in my eyes. In fact, my eyes are just about the only part of my body that doesn't hurt after what I went through. So I sat on the chair, not quite sure of what to do next, and the doctor asked me which eye was bothering me. I figured that the safest answer was "both."

"Fine," he replied, "Let's get started." He showed me a chart full of letters and numbers in different sizes, and I was supposed to tell him what I could see. I can't tell you what an easy test it was. I could see everything perfectly.

When we were finished with that, the doctor asked me if I was certain that I did not see well.

"Uh, of course, I mean of course not," I quickly assured him.

He thought about this for a while and then said, "This is what we're going to do. I want you to try on a pair of eyeglasses and tell me if they help you. If they do, you can have them."

I was delighted. If I returned to Lidingo with eyeglasses, everyone would know that this time, I wasn't joking. The doctor put the glasses on my nose and asked me if I saw well now.

"Oh, yes, doctor," I told him, "Much better."

He burst out laughing! I had never seen a Swede laugh so hard, and I had to start laughing myself. When the two of us calmed down, he removed the glasses from my nose and smiled. "Raizy," he said, "The lenses in those glasses are made out of plain glass! I wanted to be sure you see well."

Can you imagine how I felt when he said that, dear diary? I don't think I've ever been so embarrassed! How had he known? He definitely managed to pull a fast one on me! I left in a hurry and went to meet my friends outside.

At first, I didn't say anything about what had happened. But I couldn't help myself, and I told them the whole story on the way home. They laughed so hard that the people on the bus kept staring at us. I guess they were shocked at how rude our manners were.

I told Mrs. Igell everything. She didn't laugh, but at least she wasn't angry. Both of us acted as if nothing had happened. I never got around to telling you about it, because two days later I saw a little protrusion on my wrist. I kept checking to see if it was still there, but it didn't go away. It was beginning to look like I really would have to go to Stockholm, but not to have a good time.

I felt a little foolish, but I went to Mrs. Igell. She took me over to Mr. Igell and showed him my wrist. They decided that I had to go to Stockholm, where a surgeon would examine the protrusion.

This time I went by myself. A friendly doctor examined my wrist from every possible angle, and decided that I needed an operation. He checked his schedule. "Today is Thursday," he said. "We'll do the surgery on Sunday."

Was I scared! My pulse was racing so fast I could hardly get home. This was not at all what I had expected. All the way back to Lidingo, all I could think about was how they would anesthetize me, and then I would never wake up again. There had been days when I would have been glad to fall asleep and never wake up, back in the camps. Life did not mean much then. But now I was in Lidingo, and I wanted to live.

When I got back home, I staggered off the bus straight into the arms of - who else - Mrs. Igell. I told her what the doctor had said, and you wouldn't believe how reassuring she was. For one thing, she told me that Rivka was going to have a tonsillectomy on Sunday, right in the same hospital. She promised me to see to it that we would be together. Besides, she said, this really was a very minor surgery, and with G-d's help, I would be just fine; I should just make sure to pray well in the morning. I do this anyway, but you can imagine what a job I did that Sunday morning! Rivka, by the way, was very happy that I was going to be with her in the hospital.

Dear diary, as you've probably guessed, if I'm in good enough condition to be writing to you now, everything went well, thank G-d, and I woke up after the anesthetic. Now you understand why I didn't write for several days. But there's something else I have to tell you. You know how they spoil us here in Lidingo, especially the sick girls. Our friends came to visit us in the hospital every day, bringing us goodies, and, most importantly, notes from the classes we missed. It looks like they covered alot while we were away, as usual.

The Rebbetzin also came for a visit and asked if we wanted anything special. We decided that what we really missed was sour milk with sugar. This may seem strange to you, but in Lidingo this is a real treat. Of course, Mrs. Igell arrived in short order with the sour milk and sugar. We wanted to eat it right away, but were too embarrassed, because there were six other women, all strangers, with us in the room. We decided to wait until later that night.

The nurses came around to take everyone's temperature and hand out pills. Then all the patients were given supper. We ate our kosher food from Lidingo. Finally it was time for lights out. This was what we had been waiting for. Rivka and I took the sour milk out of our night table drawers, poured in the sugar, and devoured it. It was dark in the ward, and since we were quiet, no one noticed what we were doing. We enjoyed ourselves immensely. When we were done, we wished each other good night and tried to fall asleep.

Before we could, however, we saw the flashlights of the nurses, making their nightly rounds to check on the patients and replace intravenous bags. I knew that Rivka was awake, because she whispered, "It's a good thing we finished the sour milk already. Can you imagine if they would have caught us?"

I stifled a giggle, and we tried to pretend we were asleep.

Then a strange thing happened. As the nurses went from one bed to another, we heard a strange sound, something like *krip, krop, krip, krop*.

"What's that stuff on the floor?" one of them asked.

"I don't know," said the second nurse, "Maybe there's something stuck to our shoes. We'll have to check when we finish the rounds."

I pulled the blankets over my head and almost died laughing. I knew exactly what the krip, krop was. It seems we weren't careful enough when we prepared our snack in the dark, and some of the sugar spilled on the floor. The nurses had stepped on it, and...

As soon as the nurses left the ward, Rivka and I ran to the bathroom, where we laughed helplessly over the *krip, krop* and the innocence of those lovely nurses.

Fortunately, that was the end of our adventures in the hospital. Rivka and I returned to Lidingo, where everyone was happy to see us. We're already back in the swing of classes and homework, and the preparations for the *Rosh Chodesh* party. This time, since it's *Rosh Chodesh Adar*, we decided to write poems for the party about each of the teachers. Chaya has already volunteered to help us. I think Mrs. Igell is going to be the Purim Rebbetzin, and I'm sure it will be a great party.

That's it for now. I've written enough today to make up for all the days I missed, and my hand is beginning to hurt. I hope that from now on, we'll always be together.

Faithfully yours,
Raizy.

Purim Fun

Lidingo was lively all year round, but as the month of *Adar*, 1947, approached, spirits soared. The party held to celebrate *Rosh Chodesh* was wonderful. In keeping with the season, the girls took the liberty of imitating the teachers and staff. True to her word, Chaya also helped them compose Hebrew riddles about everyone, and they spent a laughter filled evening figuring them out. Here are some of the favorites:

He's always with us,
but he doesn't come often,
He takes care of everything,
Both in village and in town,
He cares for us as
a father for his son,
Now guess, what's his name? - - - (R. Chasdan)

"The son of Yaakov" in German,
"Freedom" in Russian,
A sensitive, Jewish heart,
Our rabbi and teacher - - - (Rav Jacobson)

She wants to teach Hebrew
But speaks German,
She never raises her voice,
But always bears the burden - - - (Rebbetzin Jacobson)

The riddles, based on daily life in Lidingo, were easily solved. Then the girls made up a few more of their own. This evening was only a prelude to the Purim party two weeks later.

A "Purim Rov" is a traditional part of Purim fun in the *yeshivot*. For Lidingo, Tzipora suggested the idea of a Purim Rebbetzin, and Mrs. Igell was the natural choice. Just the sight of her dressed in the Rebbetzin's clothes, which were far too big for her small frame, had the girls rolling with laughter. Mrs. Igell did a fine imitation of Rebbetzin Jacobson's gestures and intonation when she delivered a mock-serious lecture entitled "By the Rivers of Babylon," spiced with jokes about life in Lidingo. Next on the schedule was an amusing Purim fair, followed by the festive Purim dinner. The girls loved it.

* * *

Little Lenka, the youngest girl in Lidingo, also performed at the party. She put on a short skit and sang. It was hard to believe that this was the same frightened, withdrawn child who had come so unwillingly to Lidingo at her uncle's insistence, just one short year ago. Now she was one of the gang, loved, accepted, and rather spoiled - there was always someone ready to play with Lenka! Esther, who had adopted her the day she arrived, made sure she attended classes, and Lenka had learned to read, write, and do arithmetic beyond her age level.

Lenka's adjustment had been gradual. When she first came to Lidingo, no one commented on the cross she wore around her neck, or on her other strange habits, and she was not pressured to conform to the school's timetable. The Rebbetzin felt that Lenka would have to grow from within, at her own pace. At first, she had been rebellious. She overslept and was late to every meal. Esther always invited her to join her, but she refused, and she was not forced to come. Everyone would already be up and done with morning prayers and breakfast. They would all be in class, while Lenka was alone in the dormitory. Eventually, she had to admit she was lonely and bored, despite the late breakfasts and personal attention from Mrs. Igell. The constant kindness of those around her began to make its mark, and she decided to start getting up on time.

During prayers, Lenka stood on the sidelines, watching. One day Lenka asked Esther about the prayers. Esther gladly explained and taught her the words. Lenka also asked her why the other girls did not wear crosses, like hers. Esther answered carefully that the cross is a Christian symbol, not a Jewish one, so Jews do not wear it. A week later, Lenka approached Esther and whispered a secret in her ear: "Esther, I threw away my cross." She finally felt ready to part with it, not because she had been told so, but because she wanted to.

Lenka's attachment to Lidingo became apparent in a rather unfortunate incident. As it turned out, Lenka actually did have some surviving relatives after all. From time to time, she would pay them short visits. One such visit was planned to be of a week's duration. Since their room was quite crowded, Esther moved Lenka's bed out to the hall for the week. But Lenka surprised them - she was homesick, and returned a day early. When she entered the room, the color drained from her face. The girls greeted her happily, but she did not respond, not even to Esther.

"Where's my bed?" she whispered, "Who took it? Don't you want me?" She turned to Esther and asked accusingly, "Why didn't you watch my bed? Don't you want me either?"

Esther was shocked. But she understood Lenka's pain, and was anxious to reassure her. "Lenka," she said, "How can you talk like that? Come with me and

I'll show you your bed. We took it out of the room while you were away to have a little extra space, that's all. We didn't know you were coming back today. Your bed is waiting for you, and so is your spot in the room. Why, you're my best friend!" Esther said as she hugged the younger girl.

Lenka accepted Esther's explanation, but she was not entirely mollified. From then on, she checked her bed daily, to make sure it was still in its proper place. The next time she returned from a visit to her relatives, the first words out of her mouth were, "Esther, what about my bed? Is it still in the room?"

After making sure his niece was safe in Lidingo, Avraham Levi's search for relatives had led him to America. With his family's assistance, he was able to establish himself comfortably in the United States. When he returned to Lidingo to take Lenka back with him, they all realized that they would have to let her go.

Lenka cried as she said goodbye to her friends in Lidingo. Parting from Esther was especially hard. Naively, she promised that she would be back in a week! They all missed her, and were pleased when she began to write to them from America. Lenka wrote that she was happy with her uncle, and was attending an American Bais Yaakov school. She never failed to mention how much she missed them all, and that she hoped to see them again some day. Lenka's wish came at least partially true when several Lidingo girls went to America to live with relatives, and enjoyed a loving reunion with their surrogate baby sister.

Lost Souls

Life in Lidingo had its setbacks too.

At times, the girls would be overcome by a powerful need to unburden themselves, and they would sit in their rooms and talk about their experiences. These conversations generally took place at night; the silence and the darkness were somehow conducive to heart-to-heart talks. One night, Rikva told her roommates about her friend Hadassa.

Hadassa was a fine, quiet girl from a distinguished Hungarian rabbinical family. She had been in Dovers-dorp with Rivka in the days before there were Jewish schools in Sweden. There were not many Jewish families in Sweden to adopt the orphaned girls who poured into the country, but numerous Swedish gentile families welcomed them with open arms. Hadassa and Rivka had been good friends, but when a Swedish family offered to take Hadassa, they lost touch. Rivka had no idea of what had become of her.

The girls decided to tell the Rebbetzin about Hadassa; perhaps she could do something to locate Rivka's friend. The Rav and Rebbetzin traced her to a Swedish family in Stockholm, where she was enrolled in a public high school.

Chaya decided that it is important enough to try to bring Hadassa back to the Jewish community. A two hour bus trip took her to the Stockholm high school which Hadassa attended. Based on Rivka's description, she spotted her easily: a tall, beautiful seventeen-year-old girl with fair hair and blue eyes.

Chaya approached her. "Hello," she said, "Are you Hadassa?"

Hadassa did not respond. She just stared at the strange young woman in surprise.

"Excuse me," said Chaya again, "Is your name Hadassa?"

"No," the girl said coldly, "My name is not Hadassa. My name is Anita." She turned to leave.

Chaya refused to give up. Something in the girl's eyes told her she was not mistaken.

"That may be what they call you now, but I know that your real name is Hadassa." The girl did not answer. "Do you remember Rivka from Doversdorp?" Chaya continued, "She's the one who told me about you."

Now Hadassa was willing to listen; Rivka had been her best friend in Doversdorp. She agreed to go with Chaya to a nearby park, where they sat on a bench and talked. Chaya told Hadassa about Lidingo. She said that Rivka and the girls there would be delighted to have her join them.

"You don't have to worry about me," protested Hadassa, "I've been living with a fantastic family this past year. They treat me like a daughter and I have everything I want. They're really good to me."

"I'm glad to hear that they treat you so well, Hadassa, but how can you forget your origins, your past? I heard that your father was a rabbi in Hungary, and that you come from a very distinguished family. Don't you think that your place is in Lidingo, among Jews?"

Hadassa was silent. She had not forgotten her parents' home and their pious way of life. She could picture her saintly father, for whom teaching Torah and helping others was a way of life, and her wonderful mother, who was always smiling, always on the lookout for a *mitzva*. She loved them and missed them, but she loved her new family too.

"Look," she appealed to Chaya, "I understand what you're saying, but I can't do this to them. After all they've done for me, after all they've invested in me, how can I just walk out on them?"

"I'm sure they'll understand," Chaya assured her. "Thank them sincerely for all they've done for you and explain how you feel. Don't worry. You do the right thing and G-d will help you."

Hadassa nodded slowly. Chaya did not want to give her a chance to change her mind, so she accompanied her to her foster family's home. "They know me as Anita," Hadassa reminded her.

As Chaya had predicted, they accepted the news of Hadassa-Anita's decision graciously. They had grown very fond of her, but they understood her desire to be among her own people. Chaya took Hadassa with her to Lidingo, where she was warmly received. Rivka gladly took her under her wing.

"You'll see, Hadassa," she promised her, "You'll get used to Lidingo soon, and I'm sure you'll love it here. We all do."

For a while, it looked like Hadassa really had adjusted. Within a short time, she began to learn Hebrew, and as far as anyone could see, was comfortably settled in the school, socially and academically. Everything was fine, until the day she disappeared. Rivka was frantic, and ran to tell Chaya. "I just spoke to her a few minutes ago," she told her, "And now I can't find her anywhere."

The two of them went looking for Hadassa. It was Chaya who found her, sitting at the bus stop with her suitcase.

"I'm going back to my family in Stockholm," she said flatly, "They sent me money for carfare."

"But Hadassa, why?" pleaded Chaya, "Weren't you happy here with us?"

"I was."

"Then why are you leaving?"

"I lived with them for a whole year, and they were very good to me. I miss them."

"Why didn't you tell the Rebbetzin or Mrs. Igell? I'm sure they would have let you go to visit them. They would have understood. In fact, I think you should go speak to one of them right now and ask for permission to go to Stockholm. Just let them know when you plan to be back."

Instead of answering, Hadassa lowered her eyes. Chaya's kindness only made her feel worse. She really had been happy in Lidingo, and she knew it was right for her to be there. But her heart was someplace else... with someone else.

"Chaya," she whispered timidly, "I want to tell you the truth."

"Yes?"

"The family in Stockholm... they have a twenty year old son, and... I'm in love with him. That's why I want to go back."

Chaya was stunned. She hadn't even known these people had a grown son, let alone that Hadassa was involved with him. She could imagine what the poor girl was going through, torn by powerful conflicting emotions.

As she had that day in Stockholm, Chaya sat with Hadassa and talked to her about her origins. She explained to her that her feelings for the young man were actually an outgrowth of her gratitude to the kind foster family, and of her need for security and stability.

"Gratitude is a positive thing," Chaya said gently, "But in this case, the results are negative. I don't doubt that he's a fine young man, but the fact remains that he is not a Jew. Hadassa, your parents were killed because they were Jews. How can you disgrace their memory by marrying a gentile? I know you haven't forgotten them, that you still love them. Do you think this is what they would want for you? Do you think G-d spared you so that you could marry out of your faith?"

Hadassa listened, and cried. Her head knew that Chaya was right, but her heart was torn. They talked and cried some more, until finally, Hadassa decided to remain in Lidingo.

"There is something I want you to know, Hadassa," said Chaya, "We are happy that you are here with us, and we all want very much to help you. We want you to live a Jewish life, as your parents would have wished, but ultimately, the decision is yours. You do not have to come back with me now, and if you do, you are free to leave whenever you wish. It is your life. All I ask is that if you choose to leave, tell us, so that we won't worry about what's happened to you."

Hadassa followed Chaya back, knowing she had done the right thing. When she returned to her room, Rivka greeted her with obvious relief, and no one mentioned the episode again.

Unfortunately, however, Hadassa did not last long at Lidingo. Once again she disappeared, but this time she told Rivka where she was going. "I'm going to Stockholm, to my foster family. I have to speak to... him. I have to explain to him why I left, why I stayed in Lidingo. I want him to understand. I'll be back in a few days, but this is something I have to do."

Rivka watched with a heavy heart as the beautiful young girl packed her bags. Would she really come back? Wasn't she making things more difficult for herself by seeing the young man again?

Hadassa promised that everything would be fine. "Don't worry," she said confidently, "I'll be back before you know it."

But she wasn't. She stayed in Stockholm and married the son of her kindly non-Jewish foster parents. When the news reached Lidingo, it was greeted with great sorrow: a Jewish daughter had been lost to her people. No one heard from Hadassa again, not in Sweden, and not later in *Eretz Yisrael.*

Many years later, Divine providence brought Rochke and Hadassa together unexpectedly, in London. If Hadassa-Anita had not approached her, Rochke would not have recognized her. In answer to Rochke's carefully phrased questions, Hadassa mentioned that she had divorced her husband, and had not remarried. She was alone and unhappy, searching for herself in a perplexing world. She and Rochke spoke for a long time. Rochke encouraged her to return to Judaism. Hadassa did not commit herself, but she did promise to write. They shook hands warmly, and Rochke hoped that perhaps Hadassa would have a change of heart. Sadly, she never heard from her again. What became of Hadassa? No one knows.

Tragically, Hadassa's story was not unique. There were so many precious Jewish daughters, good girls from good homes, who were lonely and alone, starved for warmth, love, and security. When these needs were met by well-meaning, compassionate Swedish families, the girls accepted their overtures eagerly, and were lost to the Jewish people.

The Seder Night

It was *erev Pesach*, and the girls were up to their ears in cleaning. Not only *chometz* but dust and dirt as well were attacked with a vengeance, in the dormitories, classrooms, storerooms, kitchen, and dining room. Lidingo was expecting special guests for the holiday: the hospital patients, whom the girls visited faithfully all year long, were coming for *Pesach*. The girls had become deeply attached to their unfortunate friends, and asked Mr. Igell for permission to invite them. Following a staff meeting to discuss the logistics, he contacted the hospitals, and to everyone's delight they agreed that all the girls who were strong enough to walk could join their friends in Lidingo for the holiday.

As soon as the good news arrived, the Lidingo girls swung into action. Some two hundred guests were expected, outnumbering students and staff combined. The girls worked long hours in the kitchen, helping the cooks prepare the enormous amounts of food necessary for a crowd of that size. They willingly gave up the comfort of their own beds and their own rooms, turning them over to the guests while they slept in the dining room and storage rooms. Most of the last day before Pesach was spent carrying extra Red Cross beds to the dormitory rooms which had been lovingly prepared for the sick girls.

They arrived on *erev Pesach*, pale and tired, but very excited. The Lidingo girls welcomed them warmly, and could not do enough for them. Each of the visitors was given a bed and a cabinet for her belongings. After getting settled in the dormitories, they went downstairs to see the dining room.

It was beautiful. The tables were beautifully set with white tablecloths, with the seder plate in the center. Piles of fresh matzos, covered with decorative cloths hand embroidered by the girls, were on each table. In order to provide each of the visitors with maximum care and attention, they were seated at the tables with the Lidingo regulars on either side.

To the girls' delight, Rav Jacobson, who had traveled to the United States on behalf of the institution, returned just in time for Pesach. Unfortunately, he came home sick, but still insisted on conducting the seder for his "angels." He guided them enthusiastically through the *Haggadah*, explaining the age old concepts and ideas in a way they could all understand and appreciate. As always, the Rav included warm words of encouragement for all the girls, both his students and their guests. About half way through the seder, however, he felt so weak that he had to leave the table. Mr. Igell took over, bringing the seder to a satisfying conclusion.

For the girls, it was a poignant reminder of Pesachs past, at home with their families. For my father, Reb Nissan Yaakov Igell, it was only his fourth Pesach as an orthodox Jew.

* * *

Nissan Yaakov Igell had been born in Sweden, the third of five children. He was educated in the local public schools and went on to university, where his considerable talents were quickly recognized. He was elected Chairman of the Jewish student and youth organization in Gotborg, served on numerous other committees, and was active in the university's social life. He was held in high esteem by both students and staff, and the future looked very bright. Yet for young Nissan, this was not enough; as a Jew, he needed something more. Much as he admired the Swedish people for their honesty, order, discipline, courtesy, and other fine qualities, his soul yearned for truth. He began to research his family's past, and that of his people.

At that time, the Jewish community in Sweden was very small, and largely assimilated. Nissan was basically on his own. Then, in his father's home, he found a treasure which spurred him on: old volumes of *Mishnah*, Gemara and more, passed down for generations, but untouched for far too long. Nissan knew that his successful academic career could no longer satisfy him; he would truly find himself in his father's inheritance. His hands shook as he opened the first book, an old *Chumash*. He had much to learn, but whatever it took, his life would never be the same.

This was the beginning of Reb Nissan Yaakov's odyssey. Later he would meet Rav Shlomo Wolbe, who became a cherished teacher, guide, and inspiration. Torah became the undisputed center of Mr. Igell's life. As long as he lived, he never stopped learning, even under the most difficult conditions. He also became a staunch supporter of Torah scholars to his dying day.

When the Swedish government approved the opening of an orthodox girls' school in Lidingo, Mr. Igell was their natural choice for administrator. Not only was he an a native born orthodox Jew, a rarity in Sweden, he had outstanding academic credentials, had served with distinction as an officer in the Swedish army, and was known to be a loyal, patriotic citizen. When he was offered the job, Mr. Igell held an excellent position in a Stockholm university, and lived a comfortable, secure life in the city. He and his wife, Nina, left it all behind without a second glance, to fulfill what they perceived as a sacred duty to the Jewish people. He devoted himself wholeheartedly to the efficient running not only of the school, but of the entire program, and took personal responsibility for the wellbeing of the students and staff.

* * *

Now, under his direction, the *seder* continued uninterrupted. Everyone was involved; the girls asked questions, answered them, and sang the traditional songs. They concluded the seder with the song that stayed with them throughout the remainder of the holiday: "The Pesach seder has been properly completed... G-d's redeemed will go to Zion with song."

Most of the patients were able to stay at the table to the seder's end, participating fully. As for the rest of the holiday, it was sheer pleasure. With G-d's help, no one had to be readmitted to the hospital before Pesach was over. In fact, some of the girls felt so much better after the holiday that they refused to return to the hospital, preferring to stay on in Lidingo. Some of the physicians attending them were quite understanding and gave their approval. Even for the girls who had to leave, the visit was a great success, and the school would later receive letters of appreciation from the doctors, congratulating them on the good condition of the patients on their return. The visit had been wonderful for them, and the doctors were optimistic about their chances for a speedy recovery.

For the next two years, the seder was again celebrated in Lidingo, but 1949 saw the girls' wishes come true: they had reached the longed for shores of *Eretz Yisrael*, and spent Pesach there.

To Eretz Yisrael

The school in Lidingo functioned for three years. As they grew into young womanhood, the girls received both a well rounded general high school education and a thorough grounding in Torah studies, in an atmosphere of love and trust.

In 1948, two and a half years after the school's opening, Lidingo was granted two immigration certificates for *Eretz Yisrael*. The news was very exciting, because *Eretz Yisrael* was everyone's dream, but at the same time, it created a problem. What was a school with over one hundred students going to do with only two certificates? To waste them was unthinkable, but to whom should they be given? How could they favor any two girls over the others? They were all impatient to leave Sweden, and no one could know that a year later, after Israel's War of Independence, restrictions on immigration would be lifted.

After much deliberation, the decision was made: Batya and Nechama would be the ones to go. Both of them had relatives in *Eretz Yisrael* with whom they could live, and both were old enough to start thinking about homes of their own.

Lidingo was in a furor; two of their girls would really be making the longed for move! The others felt that even if for now they were left behind, part of them was going with their two friends. Batya and Nechama packed their suitcases with everything they owned. On second thought, they decided that it would be better to travel light, and distributed all but their most essential belongings to the other girls as mementos. These tokens of love were tearfully presented with a mixture of joy, at their own good fortune and the pain of separation.

With Batya and Nechama safely on their way, life returned to normal in Lidingo, but the atmosphere was now charged with a distinct spark of anticipation. Everyone wanted to move on, and they talked of nothing else. *Eretz Yisrael* was a major part of the school curriculum. Its history and geography were studied extensively, and Hebrew was the official language of Lidingo. Not only were the girls proud of their academic accomplishments, they also gained confidence about their future in the new land. Despite the security problems plaguing *Eretz Yisrael* in those days, they were optimistic. Every day they prayed, "And gather us together from the four corners of the earth to our land."

About six weeks after their departure, the first letter came. Almost as soon as they had reached Cyprus, they sat down to write to their sisters and teachers in Lidingo. The letter was passed from hand to hand, but with all the excitement, it was almost impossible to read it. Rivka realized that it would take hours for them all to have a turn, and suggested that she would read it aloud, so that they could all hear the news. No one uttered a sound as she read.

"Precious, beloved teachers and treasured friends, *shalom* to you all!

By now, you must have heard that we arrived safely in Cyprus on the "Chaim Arlozorov". So much happened on the way that we can't write it all now. G-d willing, we hope to be able to tell you everything in person one day soon.

We all want to express our heartfelt gratitude for the wonderful education and guidance that we received from

you. We've met people here from all over the world, including many girls our own age. Coming from Lidingo, we were surprised to see how little they'd learned after the war. We are happy that instead of wasting our time in Sweden, we spent it studying. The education we received in Lidingo made up for what we lost during the six years of the war, and we know that we have only you to thank.

Everyone in the camp, young and old, studies Hebrew diligently. Wherever we go here, we hear someone working on his Hebrew - what a beautiful sound! But then, *Eretz Yisrael* is practically around the corner, so I guess it's not that surprising. We, Lidingo girls, speak Hebrew, of course, and everyone is amazed that we learned so fast. We can also read stories in Hebrew, and even whole books.

We spend our mornings studying in the youth village here, and try to use the rest of our time well too. We all know how valuable it is. It looks like we're going to be in Cyprus for quite a while. There are 1,400 people here now, with more arriving all the time. Since only 450 certificates are issued each month, we'll just have to wait our turn. As things stand now, the only way to *Eretz Yisrael* is via Cyprus, but we're sure that G-d will help us get there soon. The conditions here are much better than we expected. Emissaries from *Eretz Yisrael* often come, to teach us and prepare us for *aliyah*. The only problem is that we miss you all terribly, and can't wait to see you again - in *Eretz Yisrael*.

What's new in Lidingo? How is everyone? The girls must have made alot of progress in their studies since we left. Please write to us about everything! Best regards to every single one of you. With warm kisses, until we see each other in our land,

Yours,
Nechama

Batya added the following:

Greetings from the girls and from everyone, including my sister. Best regards to the Chasdan family, to Miriam, and the Wassermans.

We have not forgotten what we learned in Lidingo from the Rebbetzin and all our devoted teachers. *Kashrus* is observed here, and since most of the people we came with are religious, we even have a synagogue. There is also a youth group, started by emissaries from *Eretz Yisrael*. Everyone here is impressed by how active we are and by how much we know, especially about Jewish law. Our faith in G-d sustains us during these difficult days. It helps us believe that we will soon arrive in *Eretz Yisrael*, and that we will see you there soon.

With much love and longing from all of us,

Batya.

Some time after Batya's and Nechama's departure, a number of Jewish girls elsewhere in Sweden who planned to leave the country learned that an Aliyah Bet ship, the Ulua, would be transporting refugees to *Eretz Yisrael*. Older sisters of some of the Lidingo girls were going to try their luck on the Ulua, and asked Rav and Rebbetzin Jacobson's permission to take their younger sisters along. Six girls from Lidingo left on the Ulua. Because of the nature of the trip, there was a great deal of concern for their safety. When the British seized such vessels, their passengers were interned in detention camps in Cyprus. Their friends in Lidingo anxiously awaited word that they were safe... somewhere.

It was only half a year later, when they all met in Haifa, that Shlomit told them the unembroidered details of what had happened to them on the Ulua and later in Cyprus.

"We embarked on the SS Ulua, which was actually a freighter, pressed into use by Aliyah Bet. Three decks of bunks had been installed in the hold for the passengers' use. It was impossible to sit up, and even lying down was none too easy.

"When we left Sweden, there were six hundred and fifty people crammed onto the ship. We accepted the cramped conditions and meager food graciously, but when another few hundred people came aboard in Italy, the crowding became so unbearable that we threw our belongings overboard to make room for the newcomers. It was a nightmare, but everyone felt that the ultimate goal was what really counted, not what we had to do to reach it.

"By then it was January. The sea was stormy, and it rained constantly. The deck was covered with water. Sitting in the hold was like taking a cold shower, and our thin blankets were soaked. Most of the passengers lay on their bunks, sick and exhausted. Those who felt a little better tried, not too successfully, to make them more comfortable. Then, to make things worse, the ship took a wrong turn and ended up in the Bay of Biscay, near Spain. The ocean was churning, but our ship had to stay away from the coast so that we wouldn't be noticed. If the British got wind of our plans, we were finished.

"We all just sat on our bunks like so many wet rags, too drained to move. This was our captain's finest hour, as he went from one passenger to the other, offering us food, drink, and whatever other assistance he could provide. He also promised us that he and his crew would stick with us: they would not abandon us in our time of need. With G-d's help, the ship came through the storm unharmed, and we continued on our way. But that was not all.

"A few days later, another disaster struck. It looked like this time the ship would finally go under. We must have sprung a leak, because the deck began to fill with water. It seeped into the hold, and we could feel the boat starting to settle. The crew and some of the passengers, who could drag themselves to their feet, grabbed buckets and started bailing out. Anyone who still had any sort of luggage was asked to throw it overboard. We begged G-d to save us from drowning, and with His help, we survived this crisis too.

"By now, we were eating nothing but sardines and crackers three times a day, but somehow we kept body and soul together. When we approached the coast of *Eretz Yisrael*, we were forbidden to go on deck. The ship was as silent as a grave, as it was trying to hide from the British. But it did not help, they have spotted us and in no time we were surrounded by warships. We sat packed into the hold, drenched with perspiration. We were used to the cold European climate, and we felt like the ship was on fire. The men went up to the deck to fight for our right to land, armed with the sardine cans and bottles we women gave them. They were heroes, fighting machine guns with sardine cans!

"When the British realized that our ship was unarmed, they bombarded us with tear gas. We literally didn't know what had hit us! Suddenly we couldn't see a thing, and tears started pouring from our eyes. We just couldn't stop crying, and we thought we were going blind. The injured fighters were lying on the deck, but we were powerless to help them.

"Seething with anger, the British soldiers stormed onto the ship and started manhandling the passengers. Even those who could no longer move on their own were forced onto a British ship. We all resisted, but there wasn't much we could do to stop them. To be honest, we really didn't stand a chance. The ship was anchored off Haifa for a week. We could see the lights of Mount Carmel, but as far as we were concerned, *Eretz Yisrael* could have been a million miles away.

"On the Fast of Esther, we arrived in Cyprus, expelled from the land of our fathers. The British subjected us to humiliating body searches, like criminals. If they found anything they considered contraband, they confiscated it immediately. For many of us, it was a chilling reminder of the all too recent past.

"The conditions in Cyprus were terrible. In no time, the combination of sand, heat, and sweat had produced miserable sores all over our bodies. Water was tightly rationed, and there wasn't even enough for washing. The food was meager. We burned from the heat by day and froze from the cold at night. But despite the inhuman conditions, our morale stayed high. There were classes, taught by volunteers from *Eretz Yisrael*, as well as youth clubs and social activities. The synagogue teemed with worshippers day and night.

"We Lidingo girls were a constant source of amazement. We spoke fluent Hebrew, and could converse freely on just about any topic. Our fellow internees also admired us for our strict religious observance. We spent alot of time just talking about Lidingo - about all

Lidingo girls before their *Aliya* to *Eretz Israel*

of you, about what you were learning now, about our experiences together. We never forgot where we came from.

"As much as it seemed at times that our exile in Cyprus would never end, it finally did. We arrived in *Eretz Yisrael* the day before Yom Kippur. Our first stop was Atlit, where we were received and processed by the British. They fingerprinted us like criminals, and then - only then - did they allow us to leave.

"In all our dreams of *aliyah*, we never imagined that it would be like this. But now it was behind us, and thank G-d, we were finally home, in the land of our fathers at last."

Not all the Lidingo girls went to *Eretz Yisrael*. Many went to live with relatives in America, and with the help of Rav Boruch Kaplan, principal of the Bais Yaakov seminary in Williamsburg, an additional forty girls were able to emigrate to the United States and begin new lives.

The Last Night in Lidingo

The girls sat together in the dining room around tables laden with a feast of untouched food, unable to tear themselves away and go up to their rooms. The ramshackle hut that had become their dining room, the scene of so much activity for three long years, throbbed with one unspoken word: farewell.

No one talked as they gazed at the walls of the hut and examined its white ceiling and shaky wooden floor. These were long moments of introspection, heavy with private thoughts and emotions. It was Brachie who broke the spell. She began to sing, almost to herself. As her voice rose, they all joined her in singing the beloved "Lidingo song."

Come, come, daughter of Israel,
To view the treasures of our nation.
You will see something holy and pure,
And your heart will praise G-d and His greatness.

You will find enactments and statutes,
Laws and verses from the eternal kingdom.
Then you will decide, with vigor and will,
To learn eagerly, with pride.

For the simple and lazy the garden is locked,
For the pious and wise it's a wide open field.
For the willing worker it is knowledge and wisdom,
For the steadfast builder, nobility and beauty.

Do not fear! Come forward, gracious girl,
Study the chapters, peruse the verses,
You will be granted good counsel,
And difficulties will become shining light.

First, your mind will absorb new knowledge,
You will taste delectable fruit.
Then you will teach words of Torah to others,
And hasten our final Redemption.

May it be the will of the One on High
That His people be a light to the nations,
That evil, greed, and sin shall vanish,
As man learns to bear his fellow's burden.

The previous two days had been spent visiting sick friends in the hospitals. Fortunately, most of them had already been discharged, but there were still a few girls left.

When Etika came to make the rounds for the last time, she automatically headed for Sorke's room, which she had visited so many times in the past. She knew that Sorke was no longer there; her weakened body had not been able to overcome the ravages of tuberculosis. True to her own prediction, Sorke, who had barely tasted life, was gone. Lidingo had gone into mourning when she died, and Etika still had not recovered from the blow. She looked at Sorke's empty bed, and was overwhelmed by painful memories. Her eyes filled with tears. Despite all of Etika's reassuring promises, Sorke would not be joining her in Jerusalem. But then, Etika told herself, wasn't Sorke already there, in the Jerusalem on high?

A white clad nurse wandered into the room and stood behind Etika. "Can I help you?" she asked.

Etika was startled. "Oh, no, thank you," she stammered, "I was just... I just wanted to see someone," she mumbled. It must be a new nurse, she thought, otherwise she would know. Not wanting to get involved in pointless conversation, she went out to the corridor.

"Etika, hello! I hear you're leaving soon, you lucky girl." It was Chana, a girl whose lungs were so badly damaged she could hardly breathe, let alone talk. Etika hurried to her side.

"I just wanted to tell you, on behalf of us all, that we we'll never forget what you did for us. We'll always remember the beautiful packages of sweets, and the letters, and the *mishloach manos* on Purim," Chana said.

Etika blushed. "Oh, it was really nothing, the pleasure was all ours," she replied, embarrassed. She smiled, trying to cheer her friend. "With G-d's help, you'll all be out of here before you know it, healthy and strong, and we'll meet again in *Eretz Yisrael.*"

* * *

Chana's words reminded Etika of her own early days in Lidingo, all alone. She remembered the long hours spent lingering at the post office, waiting for letters that never came. She remembered her first Purim there; how she had dreaded it! The other girls had already begun receiving *mishloach manos* packages from relatives, but Etika was one of those who received nothing - nothing was sent, because there was no one to send it.

And then one afternoon, she found a surprise on her bed: a nicely wrapped parcel bearing her name. With shaking hands, she opened it and saw a package of candy, warm stockings, and a beautiful scarf. Who could have sent it? She examined the enclosed note carefully, and the handwriting looked familiar.

"Our dear Etika! Have a happy, wonderful, delicious Purim, from the Lidingo family."

Etika had felt that she was no longer alone. She too had received a package from her relatives, from her own loving family.

Etika was not the only one. Several other girls who had no one left had received similar parcels from the Lidingo family. Their eyes shone with happiness: someone had cared enough to remember them.

Etika understood all too well how her sick friends must be feeling now that they were leaving. Throughout their long, dreary stay in the hospital, the packages and letters from Lidingo had been eagerly awaited bright spots in otherwise gray days. Who would take their place when they were gone? Etika promised herself that she would keep in touch with them from *Eretz Yisrael*. If she couldn't visit, at least the girls could look forward to letters.

* * *

Etika shook herself out of her reverie. There were still more girls to visit. After that, she had a long trip back to Lidingo, where the girls were happily packing their bags. And then - it was on to *Eretz Yisrael*.

To Zion with Song

They were really leaving Lidingo, that very day! How the girls had waited for this moment... They knew they should be happy, literally singing with joy. Instead, as if by unspoken agreement, they were all strangely silent, enveloped in sad reflection. They were leaving home, and home it truly was, in the fullest sense of the word.

They had come here as pathetic, miserable human shadows. With G-d's help, Lidingo had transformed them into proud, healthy, knowledgeable young Jewish women. They had lived, played, learned, and blossomed. In Lidingo, the overwhelming problems of young Holocaust survivors grappling with sickness and the pain of an orphaned adolescence had been met head on - and overcome. Their Jewish personalities had been molded here, in the home which had given them love, warmth, stability, and so much hope. A house is just a building, with walls and doors and windows. A home is much, much more, especially when it's filled with love and caring, giving and receiving. The home that was Lidingo was equally the product of its devoted staff and its wonderful, determined students.

They left the building slowly, one step at a time. With tearstained faces, they turned back for one last peek at the building which had served them so well for the past three years. They lingered on the lawn, where they had spent so many hours in study and talk. They could see the forest, where they had gone to pick berries. Their hearts pounded as they slowly walked away to an unknown future. All but twenty-five girls left Lidingo that day. Those who stayed behind had either personal, medical, or family reasons which kept them in Sweden awhile longer. Rav Jacobson, Mr. and Mrs. Igell, and the cook stayed with them, treating them with the same care they had bestowed on the larger group. Three months later, they too left Sweden, some to join relatives in the United States and others to join their friends in *Eretz Yisrael*.

In September, 1948, the girls reached the *ma'abarah* in Binyaminah. From there, they went on to *Beit Hachalutzot* in Haifa. This fortunate turn of events was due to the devoted efforts of Rav Yaakov Katz, of blessed memory, whose home in Haifa was open to anyone in need. He was able to acquire an abandoned Arab house, which he turned into a home for the Lidingo girls. For many of them, Rav Katz's building was to be their home until they married.

Rav and Rebbetzin Jacobson did not abandon the girls when they reached *Eretz Yisrael*. They continued to live with them and care for them, both physically and spiritually, a task they viewed as their life's mission. One of the immediate concerns they had to contend with was the disappointment of the students and even the staff when arriving in *Eretz Yisrael*. In Lidingo they had lived a full Jewish life, keeping strictly with orthodox tradition. It was a terrible shock for them to find that there were bareheaded Jews in the Holy Land who did not keep *Shabbos*, or very much else of the Torah either, for that matter. This was hardly what they had expected.

The Rebbetzin, always wise and understanding, was able to put things into perspective. She reminded them that *Eretz Yisrael* remains the same Holy Land, even if, unfortunately, not everyone living there is a G-d-fearing Jew. Now they had the golden opportunity to observe the commandments unique to life in *Eretz Yisrael*, a great privilege; the prevalence of impurity and alienation from Torah did not detract from the sanctity of the land. Rebbetzin Jacobson told her girls that they should be grateful to have reached the land of their fathers, and that it was their duty now to educate its children to follow the path of the Torah. Opportunities to do so presented themselves almost immediately.

The Lidingo girls were renowned for their fine education, excellent scholastic achievements, and fluent Hebrew. Offers of teaching positions poured into *Beit Hachalutzot*. For nine months, the girls lived in the dormitory with the Rav and Rebbetzin, working in the morning and studying in the afternoon. Then, slowly, they began to disperse. Most of them married, and the rest went to live with relatives. Even after they left Haifa, the Jacobsons continued to serve as surrogate parents. The Rav made it his business to help every one of his girls find observant, learned husbands with whom they could build new families.

Somewhat later, when the Igells and their children arrived in *Eretz Yisrael*, they were greeted happily by the former Lidingo girls. Mr. and Mrs. Igell had given them more than they could ever repay, and they were delighted to see them again.

The Jacobsons moved to Jerusalem, where the Rebbetzin's weekly lectures on *parshas hashavua* were well attended by her former students. The flurry of weddings, which was not long in coming, brought them together again and again to share in each other's joy as if it were their own.

Today, thank G-d, the Lidingo girls are the grandmothers of a new generation of observant Jews. Each new arrival is a source of pride for the Lidingo family, a new link in the tradition of their martyred ancestors.

Appendix

From the Writings of the Lidingo Girls

Diary of a Lidingo Girl

It is difficult to reconstruct memories of events which took place more than forty years ago, and even more difficult to retell them. These are not memories of distant people and places; they are memories of our own selves, of our inner lives and personal experiences.

However, with the passage of the years, we have been told that these memories should be recorded, so that they will not be forgotten by the generations to come. Perhaps we should do so even if only for our own children, to remind them of G-d's kindness to the survivors of the terrible Holocaust which swept through Europe before they were born. Let our children remember the work of His faithful emmisaries, and learn of the great spiritual heights man can reach.

If this is not a literary work by contemporary standards, so be it. I make no pretensions of being a professional author - I just want to record unembellished facts in words that come from the heart.

The following are pages from a diary I kept in Lidingo in 1945, written in the Hebrew language we all spoke then.

The Diary

I've decided to keep a diary. I've always written things down on stray scraps of paper, but yesterday, when I was in Stockholm, I bought notebooks. I want to record my thoughts now, so that years later, I'll be able to compare them with my memories, and really remember...

Thursday

How I thirst for knowledge! I devour the words of the teachers like soup after a fast day. I want so much to learn, to know how to behave. Father in Heaven, I'm sure that You will have compassion on me and help me be a decent human being.

Friday

After class today, I learned a very meaningful poem by Rav A. Kaplan, of blessed memory, called "I".

Yesterday the teacher took my notebook, and in the morning she returned it, sighing, "Full of sadness." I was surprised, because I didn't think there was anything sad in my notebook. I wonder what she meant?

Motzei Shabbos

Havdalah was over a few minutes ago, and I can't wait to write. We had a wonderful class on the *mishnah* in *Pirkei Avos*, "If I am not for myself." We learned that every person has to wait for his "moment," and delve into his inner self. Everyone has to discover his own good attributes, develop them, and live the right kind of life. Our father Avraham's chief attribute was *chesed* - lovingkindness. He embraced the whole world with lovingkindness, and in return, G-d treated him with lovingkindness. Man has to search for his own "I", find the good and sublime in his character, and develop it.

At times I sense emptiness within myself. Everything seems so small and petty, and man so worthless. This is the "I for myself" the *mishnah* talks about, a man alone: so weak, so helpless. At every step he needs help from others, both from friends, and above all, from the

Al-mighty. The moment described by Rav Kaplan in his book "*Ikvos Hayirah*" is one of clarity, in which the knowledge of "If I am not for myself" and that of "When I am for myself" become one. I know I didn't explain it well, but I really do understand what he means.

Today's class was different for me for some reason. At any other time, I'd be able to listen to the Rav talk all day and all night, but today, I felt that I couldn't absorb another word. Mentally, I begged him to stop so that I could digest what he had said so far and understand it.

After class, I lay down, thought for a while, read the poem "I", and then fell asleep. I woke up when the girls came in with the mail.

Last night I was at the Rebbetzin's *Chumash* class. She said that we were shouting out loud, and she recognized my voice as well. I've decided to try not to shout any more.

Sunday

I was in the Rebbetzin's class. Now I understood the ideas of Rav A. Kaplan, of blessed memory, about opening one's eyes and seeing the Hand of the Creator in everything. All of us here were blind until our eyes were opened. The Rebbetzin talked about a different, more sublime level of vision which ordinary people never attain, not even after their eyes are opened. It's a spiritual, not material, kind of vision.

Yesterday the Rebbetzin called me over and read my composition on "Life and Death Are in the Hands of the Tongue" aloud. She said it lacked content, not because I did not have the ability to express myself, but because I did not get to the heart of the matter.

Tuesday

I read a really interesting book today. I almost felt as if I were back home. I also received a letter and a photograph from my uncle.

Sabina got news of her sister. I was so happy for her! G-d does not abandon us - that's for sure.

Monday evening

We are in the kitchen. Chana, Sima, and I are baking for the sick girls.

Something is weighing on my heart. I haven't cried for a long time. At times, incomprehensible sorrow builds up, and the only way to melt it is with tears, but you can't always cry.

Chanukah

The candles are burning. The flame rises and falls, contracts and flutters. The trees outside are bare; their branches reach for the Heavens like outstretched arms, praying.

We are preparing a presentation for the guests. The teacher asked which I would rather recite, Rav Kaplan's poem "I", or a poem of my own. I told her that I would rather do my own, because if I were to recite Rav Kaplan's poem, I might not be able to express his ideas properly. She thought that my own poem might make me sad, but I just laughed.

The day of the presentation. The guests are due to arrive in two hours. We are already all dressed up, but my heart's not in it. I'd be happy to find a quiet corner where I could sit and read a chapter of *Nach* or go over some *Chumash*.

Thank G-d, the presentation is behind us. It was a tremendous success and everyone was very pleased. We are happy that our teacher Chaya's efforts were not in vain. In fact, everything exceeded our expectations. R. Yisrael Chasdan raised 350 *kronor* for the playbills that we prepared. Rav Shlomo Wolbe spoke beautifully. The best part was our teacher's speech. All she said was, "Our girls," but with so much feeling and so much love that it was like a drop of honey in our hearts.

It's evening now. It's dark outside, but inside our room it's light and warm. Our white beds stand in two rows, five in one row and six in the other. Some girls are already in bed. Others are sitting in a different room, doing mending. Some of the girls are reading the Yiddish book we got today from R. Chasdan. What a lovely language it is, and what beautiful poems!

Everyone is busy; I'm the only one just sitting around. Even thinking is too hard for me now. It seems to me that my heart is empty. I long for... what? What am I to do? How can I fill the void within me? Perhaps I should ask the Rebbetzin tomorrow. She is so wise, I'm sure she will advise me. I think I can go to sleep now.

Tuesday, midday

I received your picture, Tatte. It isn't a good one. I look at it so hopefully: please, tell me something! Your expression is so silent, so worried. What would you say if your fatherly eyes were really looking at me now? What were you thinking then, seated in your chair?

Perhaps you were worried about how you would manage to buy winter shoes for us all. Maybe you were figuring out how to get us released from school early on Fridays. Or maybe you were just tired after a sleepless night, and that's why your eyes look so sad?

Can you see me, Tatte? Do you know that I'm alive? Does it make you happy? That's what you wanted! Or maybe you're crying for me...

Please don't worry about me. G-d, Who you taught us from childhood to love with all our hearts, and in Whom you trusted even in the face of death, saved me. Tatte, I can see you next to me and I can hear your voice. The picture is not a good one, but that doesn't matter. For me, you will always be a special, lofty figure, guiding me through life. For me, you aren't gone - you'll always be with me.

Wednesday evening

Today the Rebbetzin taught us in Chumash class why Yitzchak's eyesight failed. There is a midrash that at the time of the Akeidah, the angels wept and their tears, which fell into his eyes, dimmed his vision. I thought that perhaps when he reached this sublime spiritual level, his inner vision also became more exalted, so that earthly eyesight became superfluous.

Monday, midday

My aspiration to love all the girls has been realized to some degree. I love them all together and each one separately, because of their sweetness, their smiles, and their suffering... How I wish I could bestow some warmth on each of them - they need it so desperately!

I am waiting for the teacher. I was supposed to study with her at three, but she hasn't come yet. I recall the Rav's words about the different ways of serving G-d. Moshe was called G-d's servant, because a servant, who is constantly at his master's side, knows everything about him.

I really need a *Tanach* with *Rashi's* commentary, because without it, I don't understand a thing. How can I get hold of one?

Lately, I've become so attached to the Rebbetzin that I can't imagine living without her. How much light and life she's put in my heart!

Wednesday

On Monday evening Rav Wohlgelernter arrived with Rav Jacobson.

Chaya, our teacher, got some bad news about her husband and she didn't feel well afterwards. The next day, both of the teachers had to go away with the Rebbetzin, so the Rav taught us *dinim* and *Chumash*. The *Chumash* class was about Yaakov's blessings to his sons. In the evening, I went to the Rebbetzin's class on the Song of the Sea in *Chumash Shmos* The *midrash* says that the Jews reached such a high spiritual level that they were able to point their fingers and say, "Here is my G-d." They were inspired to establish a dwelling place for G-d's spirit in their own selves. I found this class very satisfying.

Thursday evening

Yesterday I was in the hospital. I went with the Rebbetzin, and on the way she told me that she loves to study Navi Yeshaya, and wants her children to learn it as well. She is sorry that they learn too little. What can we say?

Today, I waited all morning for class to begin. Afterwards, Sara came and announced that since the teacher doesn't feel well, class is postponed till after supper.

Sometimes it seems to me that the teacher is not happy with me. I can't always concentrate and I walk around a lot. At times I feel that I am insulated from everything that happens in the world around me, that I simply don't care.

I haven't written in my diary for a week. I've been having very bad headaches. One of the girls in the next room suddenly got sick. It's some kind of sleeping sickness; she is unconscious but she talks all the time.

Thursday

We had a class with Rav Wolbe, and then with the Rebbetzin. I felt good, really happy. I even wanted to sing! Well, maybe not to actually sing or talk, but to smile and greet everyone cheerfully, to tell them what is in my heart. When I got up this morning I was so sad, but now I'm very happy. What a great kindness! Blessed be G-d Who gladdens mourners and straightens the bowed.

Wednesday morning

Another day. Yesterday the Rav wanted to speak to me. He gave me regards from the teacher and told me that I would be studying with him in the afternoon. When I began to read the verses about atonement, I got depressed, and said that the Jews could be granted atonement for the sin of the Golden Calf, because that was a sin between man and G-d; if one sins against another person, the injustice has been done and can not be negated. The Rav told me a parable which proves that a person and his Evil Inclination are two distinct entities which can be separated. Afterwards, when I told him about my bad behavior yesterday, he advised me not to despair of working on myself. He said I should keep trying and have lots of patience. This really encouraged me and also calmed me.

Later

It's already after Pesach. The holiday was a big success, and everyone was very pleased. Our sisters, the girls who came to Lidingo from the hospitals, felt that we care about them, think about them, hope and pray for their recovery, and were happy to host them. We really are one family, no less close than sisters born to the same parents. This is a fact and we all felt it.

Iyar

The Rebbetzin told me something today. The Torah portion of Chayei Sarah tells about Eliezer's mission to find a wife for Yitzchak. Eliezer is called the servant of Avraham. Even though he did many things by himself, based on his own intelligence and understanding, he is still called his master's servant. Most servants feel at liberty when they leave their master's presence, especially if they can act on their own, as if they are in control of the situation. Not Eliezer - he didn't even mention his own name.

I think a lot about my spiritual standing. For the most part, I am sad. At times everything seems hazy and far away. Crying is an everyday occurrence, brought on by any trifling incident. At times I'm choked by my tears, and at times they stream from my eyes, and I'm helpless to stop them. The only thing that keeps my spirits up are our classes - with G-d's help, they help me hold on. They rebuild the world I lost and give me the will to live, so that I can fulfill my Creator's will. I'm usually happy after class, or when I have the chance to do a mitzvah. This is a great comfort to me.

On the other hand, I can't help but think that there are so many people who are good to me, and that so much time and effort is being invested in me. Am I allowed to accept these enormous gifts? Isn't it like stealing? Once Hella told me that it takes her a long time to do her homework, because she isn't talented. And I seem to need additional private teaching to correct my poor *middos*.

Wednesday afternoon

We had a wonderful class in *Pirkei Avos*, on the *mishnah*, "If one's wisdom takes precedence over his fear of sin, his wisdom does not endure." I couldn't take notes, but afterwards the Rebbetzin took me for a walk in the forest. She repeated the whole thing and asked that I really try to understand it properly. I felt that I had received a gift which I didn't deserve. She spoke to herself, and I had the privilege of listening. I'm sure I didn't understand much of what she said, but the walk still left a lasting impression on me.

Tuesday

We are in Tomelilla, working in the fields during the day, and going to class at night. On Friday and Shabbos we learned about "And you shall eat to satiation." Rashi explains that there will be "a blessing within the stomach" - even a small amount of food will be filling. The Rav spoke about the concept of eating for the sake of Heaven. How can one achieve such a level? I, of course, did not know that one must have the proper intentions when making the blessings before and after eating. During the Shabbos meals I looked at the bread, and I truly felt G-d's blessing in every little piece. My heart overflowed with joy.

After the meal, we learned about taking interest. At times, it is easier for a person to give something as a gift than to lend it, since it goes against man's grain to do a complete favor. When a person gives a gift, he enjoys feeling that he is generous, a pleasure he doesn't have when he just lends someone something. Therefore, when he lends something, he wants to make a profit, and asks for interest.

In the evening, before *Shabbos* was over, we had a class on *Pirkei Avos*, about "One whose fear of sin is greater than his wisdom." This time I understood, which made me happy.

There was no class on Sunday. I went to the hospital in the afternoon with S. and Z. The girls were happy. Olli is much better, thank G-d. Shoshana also feels better. It was almost evening when we got back, and we found that lots of guests had arrived, including Mr. Chasdan, who came to say goodbye. We were very sorry to learn that Rozi has to go back to the hospital. Our beloved Rozi came down to the dining room with us and we all sang together. Then the car came. The Rebbetzin kissed her like a mother and sent her off with a warm blessing.

A year has already passed since we met Rav Wolbe in Doversdorp. By what merit are we privileged to be near him? Do we appreciate this enough?

Six weeks have passed in Tomelilla, and we are about to return home, back to our precious Lidingo! How we love you!

We're home. Our beloved sisters greeted us very happily. After we finished eating, I went to sleep for a while, and then, after *Minchah*, I went to the seashore to study. Everything has grown wild, the weeds along with all kinds of flowers and fruit trees. Never was I so aware of the beauty of nature as I was then. The blue and white of the sky were reflected in the clear, tranquil sea. How great is Your handiwork, O G-d!

Sunday

We had a class in our room, since Y. is in bed. At eight o'clock, a new girl came. She had been staying with a Christian family in Landskrona. Before she came, the Rav called me and said that we should go out to meet the car and give her a nice welcome. It seems that on the way over, she changed her mind about leaving her foster family, and may want to go back to them. I went out with L. and P. and we gave her a big reception. Then we went to the kitchen, but it was locked. I climbed through the window and let the other girls in. We brought her tea and something to eat, but there wasn't any sugar. G. and I ran to ask Henia, who said that Mrs. Igell has the key to the storeroom, and we had to go back.

Monday evening

I just got back from the Green Hall, where we had important visitors from *Eretz Yisrael*. They came to discuss our *aliyah*. One of them, a very pleasant looking man, asked what we planned to do in *Eretz Yisrael*. All the "sisters" looked at me, and so did he. He explained that this was something they had to know, so that they could make the necessary arrangements for the new olim. I didn't know what to say, and he got angry. He'd heard that we spoke Hebrew very well; didn't we understand his question? He had talked to much younger children, seven- and ten-year-olds, and they had answered immediately. I saw that we would have to say something, if only to be polite. I told him, "When I was seven I could also answer any question right away, a different answer every time."

In the end, he said he would send someone else to talk to us in a few days, who would then let him know what we had decided. After they left, we asked the Rav what we should say. He explained to us that we were the only ones, not only in Sweden, but possibly anywhere, who were receiving instruction from such great people. In crucial times such as ours, we should feel obligated to pass on what we had learned to others less privileged. This is a time for action, he said. We have to learn in order to teach others. He quoted the verse, "I will raise the cup of salvation, and call out in the name of G-d." When we lift our cup of salvation, we must also call out in G-d's name. We have incurred a great debt, which must be repaid.

Your Lovingkindness in the Morning

One of the girls relates:

King David (others say Moshe Rabeinu), of blessed memory, saw a prophetic vision of the long exile which the Jewish people would have to endure, which was compared to night. But our own exile, the one we witnessed and personally experienced, was the darkest and longest ever in the history of our nation.

Throughout the misery and the suffering, my dear sister Itta Masha, of blessed memory, always saw a glimmer of light: G-d's lovingkindness. She attained a very high level of faith and trust in G-d. I learned from her, but I never equaled her. In the end, her faith was rewarded. She always promised me that "we'll get out of this yet," and she was right. We were liberated and brought to Sweden.

Sweden is a cold country. Although the wonderful Swedish people showered us with love and warmth, we longed to see a fellow Jew. We thirsted for the spiritual heritage of our beloved parents.

The first Jew I saw in Sweden was Rav Jacobson, who spared no effort to go anywhere he might find Jews. He was not a young man, but he devoted his entire life and sacrificed his health for the survivors of the camps. He did everything in his power to help them, materially and spiritually. The first step was the provision of kosher food. Next came structuring an appropriate setting in which they could live as orthodox Jews. None of this came easily, and government cooperation was essential, but Rav Jacobson refused to be daunted by the difficulties.

A few weeks after our arrival in Sweden, we were brought to a place called Lovo, where there were already many other Jews. Among them was my cousin Sara, who is much older than me. She encouraged me to live a Torah life. I also met a girl my own age in Lovo, Raisa, who became a lifelong friend.

And then one day, after we had despaired of any future in this cold land - a heavenly angel appeared to rescue us. It was Rebbetzin Jacobson. When this wonderful woman came to Lovo, she actually looked like an angel! We were afraid to approach her, so she came over to us and began talking. I cannot describe the emotions she aroused in us then. She dedicated her whole life to us, to restore what we had lost and give us what our own parents could unfortunately no longer provide.

The third person I met was Rav Shlomo Wolbe. He too was an angel from Heaven, who did his utmost for the survivors, especially for the sick girls who remained in the hospitals for years. He spared no effort to visit them in the most out-of-the-way locations, encouraging them and boosting their morale.

These three angels saved us not only from physical hardship, but also from spiritual hazards, the good intentions of gentile Swedish families in particular. They overcame enormous hardships to create a warm haven for us in Lidingo, a name which will be recorded in the annals of Jewish history, never to be forgotten. This small island far away in the Baltic sea was privileged to be home to a glorious Jewish community. As Rav Wolbe once explained to us in Tomelilla, some remote locations have the merit of being associated with G-d's Name. This was the case with Lidingo.

The house in Lidingo was unique, one of a kind anywhere after the war. The educators there molded new human beings. They breathed new souls into us, carrying on where our parents had been forced to leave off. Above all, they taught to perpetuate the unbroken chain forged by the dedication of our ancestors and our beloved parents.

Glossary

Aida Hachareidis: a strictly orthodox community based in Jerusalem

Akeidah, Akeidas Yitzchak: Biblical Binding of Isaac

Aktion: rounding up of Jews for deportation

alef-bais: Hebrew alphabet

aliyah: immigration to Eretz Yisrael

Aliyah Bet: illegal immigration to Eretz Yisrael prior to the founding of the State of Israel

Baal Shem Tov: Rabbi Yisrael Baal Shem Tov, founder of the Chassidic movement

Baruch Dayan Emes: blessed be the true judge

Baruch Hashem: thank G-d

bikur cholim: visiting the sick

bli neder: a promise without taking an oath

cheder: Hebrew school

Chumash: Five Books of Moses

Chumash Shmos: Book of Exodus

chometz: leaven

dinim: Jewish law

Eretz Yisrael: Land of Israel

erev: eve

Gehenom: hell

Haggadah: text of the seder

Havdalah: ceremony marking the end of the Sabbath

Jude: Jew

Kaddish: memorial prayer for the dead

kapo: work supervisor in Nazi concentration camp, usually Jewish

kasher: make kosher

Kol Nidrei: prayer recited as the fast of Yom Kippur begins

krona, kronor: Swedish currency

latkes: pancakes

lashon hara: slander

Lecha Dodi: prayer welcoming the Sabbath

ma'abarah: transit camp

Maoz Tzur: traditional Chanukah song

mazal tov: congratulations, good luck

Mesillas Yesharim: a classic work of Jewish ethics

mezuza: parchment scroll containing Biblical verses, affixed to the doorpost of a Jewish home

middos: character traits

mikveh: ritual bath

Minchah: afternoon prayers

mischling: of mixed ancestry

mishloach manos: food packages exchanged on Purim

mishpacha, mishpachat: family

mitzvah: good deed, positive commandment

Motzei Shabbos: Saturday night after the conclusion of the Sabbath

mussar: ethics

Nach: Prophets and Writings

Navi: Prophets

Navi Yeshaya: Book of Isaiah

netilas yadayim: ritual hand washing, as upon arising or before eating bread

olim: new immigrants to Eretz Yisrael

parshas hashavua: weekly Torah reading

peyos: sidecurls

Pirkei Avos: Ethics of Our Fathers

rav, rabbanim: rabbi, rabbis

rebbetzin: rabbi's wife

rechilus: idle gossip

Rosh Chodesh: first day of a new month

Rosh Hashanah: Jewish New Year

seforim shafeh: bookcase

Selichos: special prayers, in this instance those recited daily before and during the High Holiday period

seudah mafsekes: final meal before fast

Shabbos: Sabbath

shalom: a greeting. Also: peace

Shalom Aleichem: song welcoming the angels before the Sabbath evening meal. Also: welcome

shechitah: ritual slaughter

sheva brachos: week of celebrations following a wedding

Shma Yisrael: affirmation of faith in one G-d, recited daily and before death

shochet, shochtim: ritual slaughterer(s)

Shomer Hatzair: a secular, irreligious ideological movement

siddur: Jewish prayer book

tallis: prayer shawl

Tanach: Bible

Tatte: Father

tefillin: phylacteries

treife: non-kosher

Tehillim: Psalms

Umschlagplatz: deportation center

Vaad HaHatzalah: Rescue Committee

Viduy: confession

yahrzeit: anniversary of death

Yamim Noraim: High Holidays

Yerushalayim: Jerusalem

yid: Jew

zloty, zlotys: Polish currency

Made in the USA
Monee, IL
29 August 2025